Not For Nuttin'

A Journey with
some folks without homes
"the homeless" and me.

RICHARD HENDRICK

DEDICATION

To Annie, who once again has brought me to a good thing.

TABLE OF CONTENTS

INTRODUCTION

Gus Leady, shortly before he died from another overdose, told me to write this book. *Just like that.* Gus was a man who blurted things out. After a few hours of our getting to know one another, he said to me, "Ritchie, you see so much, you gotta write a book. Ritchie, tell people – bottom line - not for nuttin'!" I decided to do it. *Just like that.* I told Gus that I would be calling it "Not for Nuttin', an expression that he closed every sentence with. Every blooming sentence. His smile expressed approval at my choice; his lack of words – a rarity - spoke of his puzzlement. I trust that you will not be puzzled. I hope that you will enjoy these vignettes and will see that the gift of your simple presence - in your various ways - to those who we call "homeless" is bottom line, not for nuttin'. And a note on "confidentiality": As a social worker I am obliged to keep confidences; as a writer I need to write, as one who has witnessed an important social reality, I want to give a picture. I am confident that confidences have been honored.

And so …"Presence is truly one of the best gifts we can offer to others in need. The value of presence to another person should not be understated. When we sit with people in the darkness and 'help them cry' we model hope and new possibilities in ways even we sometimes don't realize." Snow falling on Snow by Robert Wicks.

Rat Feces Found in Leo's Food

I, like the others, could not resist getting into the outside lane of the rotary traffic to grab a look at the message on the large cardboard sign held up by a scruffy man. Surely one of mine! George! His sign read, "RAT FECES FOUND IN LEO'S FOOD". What the hell does he mean! I parked my truck, put on my quirky hat and ID and went over. "George, Leo's going to be pissed; he gives you guys breaks - two eggs, bacon, refill on coffee, dress as you like, two bucks. 'Rat Feces Found in Leo's Food'? That's strong George, someone's going to try to lock you up."

"He's a shit head and they can't lock me up - free speech; and I'm nuts - reasonable accommodations, American with Disabilities Act, I looked it up." "So what happened?" I said, "I thought you liked Leo, everyone likes Leo". I noticed the cars were now backed up on the rotary; the sign was getting *lots* of attention. "Pills George, I think we should be talking pills. What happened?"

"He said that I worked good; that he could use me to clear the tables, that he'd give me $20 bucks at closing. He asked me not to talk to the customers. *Well excuse me!* But I didn't talk to them. That was yesterday. He wasn't there at closing and he wasn't there this morning – he skipped town, with my $20 bucks. Deliberate, gone, planned it that way, had no intention to pay me. He is gambling somewhere with my $20 bucks, and losing! So I'm telling. "Rat Feces Found in Leo's Food"

"That's nuts George, remember where you go without the medicine - you're going there. See these cars slowing down, backed up - they're reading the sign, *very effective* sign George. Leo is going to be *very* angry. When did you see rat feces in any food?"
"I saw a mouse yesterday; same thing, same thing as a rat; a mouse is just a rat without a tail. And where there is a mouse and food you got feces in food - not good, public health hazard, safety issue, needs to be reported - bingo!"

"Pills George, how long have you been off them?" George and I talked – street homily # 12: "What happens when you go off your meds and put up signs." In time, he once again agreed that perhaps -just perhaps- he was sliding and that he should get back on them.

The next day I had reason to be at the rotary again, George was there - with a sign. Again I got into the outside lane. "No more Rat Feces Found in Leo's Food."

And so … there's a lot to say about mental illness, but best that it be kept off cardboard signs.

Inspector Sherlock

"And don't forget my birthday tomorrow Sherlock" -he calls me Sherlock after the detective. "You're always walking the streets, looking around, hot on the trail of someone". It took a long time for Miguel to accept that I was a good sleuth; it took me no time at all to know that I liked his style.

"Sherlock, come here, she needs help. I called those people, told them that her fake leg is hurting her real bad, they said they would come out, they haven't. Let's go Sherlock, call them, give 'em hell". So I did, on the spot, gave them hell, my style, simply because he told me to - Miguel has that way about him. "Good, thanks Sherlock, I'll stay with her and make sure she is there when they come - and I'll tell you if they don't come" "And don't forget my birthday tomorrow - 50, I've lived that far, amazing"

I thought: I can't get him cigarettes - unhealthy - and he's diabetic so no chocolate. I found a gift that I could live with — a one-dollar lottery ticket. Miguel was waiting at the bus stop. I gave him the ticket and pulled away watching him begin the scratch and reading my birthday greeting: "Good Luck Dr. Watson, Happy Birthday, Holmes."

And so …some of my friends of the street are just waiting — waiting for a situation in their life to change, waiting for a loved one to change, waiting for them to change, waiting to win the lottery. I am reminded of the Serenity Prayer: Lord Grant me the serenity to accept the things that I cannot change, the courage to change what I can and the wisdom to know the difference.

Winken, Blinken and Nod

"Winken, Blinken and Nod one night, Sailed off in a wooden shoe-Sailed off on a river of crystal light, Into a sea of dew."
Eugene Field – 1850-1895

These are the ones that you have seen on my streets and have said, "why are these old men homeless?. How can this be in America." Old men who have chosen to spend too many days and nights on tough streets-and yes there is the matter of the booze. They soon shall..."sail off in a wooden shoe" – a good thing I think. Winken, Blinken and Nod and I, we have had our moments and I'm okay with their upcoming journey.

Winken can't walk any more and that's the only way now that the nursing home would take him. He always walks out on them. It just happened one day, no strength left in his toothpick legs. So they captured him, and yes I did the dastardly deed of getting the involuntary admission - threw the net over him. He still tries to bolt from the nursing home, tries hard to get back to his stool at Flaherty's, the only bar left in the city that will serve him. For you see, Winken has habits that are "difficult"– a kind word "difficult". Hell, even bar buddies stay away from him. A lot to do with the colostomy bag always breaking. Combined with him being drunk. He keeps trying to break out of the home, keeps falling, keeps forgetting that he falls - or not caring - and tried again.

On this day that I visit, he has given up the pursuit and is bitching and yelling for a cigarette. To silence him, the attendants wheel him downstairs, park him outside, light his cigarette and leave him. Done very quickly. I sit next to him while he smokes. I am amazed at the mileage that he can get from a cigarette and am sure that it's his finger that he ends up smoking. And on this day, on this planet, he turns to me and says, "Let's talk". For over five years, he has not said, "boo" to me or to anyone else. Now he wants to chat. We have come to our moment!

Long ago Winken forgot how to converse, so I ask questions. With no emotion his answers are "yes" and "no". "Do you think that you are dying?" Would you like me to contact any family?" "Are you in any pain?" "Do you want a priest?" "Do you miss drinking? "— (I can't believe I asked that!). And then a statement: "Someone will be with you, you will not be alone". Before I left that day I spoke with a caring nurse, she assured me that she would be with him at the hour of death. I will try to be there too.

Blinken. Don't be stupid by getting anywhere near Blinken. You'll get blind- sided with his thrusting cane. If you are new to the shelter, your friends will have fun with you; they will maneuver you close to Blinken and laugh when you are attacked. *Attacked*. Before you go to sleep make sure that someone has gotten his cane from him, if not, sleep with one eye open. Blinken is nasty - always - like that dog behind the chain- linked fence with the sign that says, "Beware of the Dog — *really!*". His brain is locked on wet. He was seated outside the nurses' office one night; isolated from the others, denied a bed in punishment, placed on a cold metal chair. I am drawn to pathos. Keeping a distance, I decided to question:

"So Blinken, were you born in Springfield?"

"What the hell do you mean, certainly - Hungry Hill"

"Any brothers or sisters? "

"For Christ sake, yeah twelve of us, up on Hungry Hill, poor as church mice without a church.

"I bet you've seen big changes since you were a kid"

"Hell yea, ain't the same."

We talked for twenty minutes – my moment with Blinken

They call *Nod* "Speedy". He shuffles. He calls himself "Ritchie Rich", "Satan", "Magruder", "Fast Charlie" and "Atta Pepper" - or something like that. We think that he has a real name but I am drawn to "Atta Pepper"- or something like that. Seventeen years in the Navy he says, but it does not check out; I wish that it did, it would make it easier for me to get him off the streets. Sometimes he'll say, "Hi guy" to me ; the rest is mumbles. He wears an elfin smile- he looks like an elf, an elf whose pants are always about to fall off. Often he is delirious, maybe Alzheimer's - probably booze.

All are amazed that Nod can find his way anywhere and more amazed that he gets from point A to point B - It takes "Speedy" forever. We are less concerned now that this brutal winter has passed. The standard in this state for commitment is "danger to self or others"; if it were "in need for care", we could get him to a safe place. Yet, this is where he wants to be now. In the middle of this past winter I asked Nod if he would allow me to look into a nursing home. I was surprised. "O.K. Guy". We had our moment and then too quickly, spring came and he sprang - wanted no part of it. I hope that he sails away before next winter.

"Winken, Blinken and Nod one night, Sailed off in a wooden shoe - Sailed off on a river of crystal light, into a sea of dew."

And so …Mother Theresa told a gathering that we need not go to Calcutta to serve; that in the United States we have so many people who are lonely. When you are old and live on the streets of America, you must be damn lonely.

Joe

"I know it's a boy's name, but it's Joe. 'J-O-E'- not 'JO' or 'Josephine'. J-O-E. They wanted a boy. I don't need a social worker." She said it without meanness and meant it. I found her intriguing. Even in her dazed places of mental illness - more so in her dazed places of mental illness - she showed strength and resilience.

I was surprised to see J-O-E back at the shelter with her baby. With others, I gathered and gazed upon the infant. A beautiful boy. Not the beautiful of all infants-*truly* beautiful! J-O-E named him Francis, "After that Saint" she told me. But how would she care for this saintly child?

J-O-E was ever attentive; Francis thrived, he was vibrant. I never saw him cry, never heard him whine; never saw him irritated or overactive. The passing around alarmed me. The worlds of those without homes were always coming up to J-O-E and her child and many wanted to hold Francis. J-O-E easily gave the baby up. On the streets and in the busy soup kitchens, passed around. It was when someone drunk stumbled with Francis that I felt a responsibility to say something

"Do you think it's a good thing to pass Francis around?"

"I want him to be comfortable with other people, I want him to go to them easily, lots of them". Someday I may not be able to take care of him."

When I heard of her death last week I recalled how she always walked in the streets as if she owned them-flaunting her dignity. Daring them to defeat her fifteen years of spirit. It was at dusk, the man was not going fast. Francis was not with her.

And so...J-O-E adored her child. Do I judge? Do I say that love is not enough that children should not be on the streets? But they are on streets and they are loved!

The Pigeon Catcher

Iowa catches pigeons. For chunks of time, he sits on the wall of the shelter and plies his craft. He casts out a long string with a loop at the end and waits. At the right moment, he jerks the string. He has told me, "It's all in the wrists and it's near impossible". I know the diagnoses: "schizoid personality disorder", and I know that Iowa will always have a tough time in this world; know that he will always be a loner, know that his presence scares people. On this day something was up, Iowa was more sullen than usual, and that is sullen! "Wha's up?" He answered, "Can't get it renewed, the license for the cab, she don't like me". I offered to go with him, to present his case to the police bureaucrat. Iowa thought about the offer. "No", he said, "every year I need to go back to reapply, got to get her to like me, need to be patient - like catching pigeons. I do catch them you know - and then I let them go"

And so ...I am reminded of the biblical: "And I will make you fishers of people"

෨

Death Be Not Proud

"I want to catch up with you, to visit you in your part of Heaven. To walk over whenever I'd like and be with you. You remember the noose - I still have it. I just got out of the hospital - the pancreas again - again they said that soon I'll die if I don't stop drinking. I believe them now. And they said that they wouldn't see me again until 30 days pass; they call me 'a frequent flyer'. What if it is really bad before 30 days are up, will they let me die on these streets?

"You know I can't stop. Sometimes it hurts bad, the pain on my left side; but what really hurts - I've never had this kind of hurt - is not having you next to me. I still see beautiful things around me: like the little flowers, and the spiders, the blueberries on the vine behind the dumpster. And our great Mother Weeping Willow tree, she still bends down and gently touches me when I sleep; she used to touch us both, remember ? Nineteen years is a long time, you and I on these streets. I got mugged last night, the first time in nineteen years - cause you were not with me. Didn't have a chance, couldn't even get to my "Staff of Justice" stick. I was sleeping it off. I remember how many times you saved me. The time I almost drowned; you came to me, brought me in, I held on. And the fire - I would have slept through it.

"I have lots of friends but no one like you. I care for people, even all the ones that have left me - but not the same way I cared for you. I *loved* you. Damn cancer!, why can't they find a cure ? First your spleen then the rest of you. I really miss you … real bad. Sparky, I don't want to be on these streets anymore without you! A lot of people tell me that I should get another chocolate lab — but I can't."

And so … I used to think solely about how "homeless people" die on the streets; I have come to know that people without homes also experience others who die on the streets: their friends, their relatives … their dog.

Do *Not* Interrupt or God
Can Find Me on the Floor

"Do not say anything, DO _NOT_ INTERRUPT!". His first words
to me. He immediately let me know that I would only be using
my listening skills …I hate it when I can only use my listening
skills. "Fifteen years in prison and I've been out twenty- five
days. I've gone to AA meetings on the outside, amazing. Me, AA
meetings! And I put myself in charge of making the coffee, and I
read the traditions, *read* in front of everyone! Do you know how
impossible that is for me?"

I jumped in the direction of an empathic social worker: "Yes
but…" "DO _NOT_: INTERRUPT! Prison did me good. When I
was a kid, I'd walk on the other side of the street so I would not
have to talk to anyone. You can't do that in prison, you gotta face
things. I didn't care about anything or anybody in prison, I was
in the hole a lot. I told guards what I thought of them. They said
I was mental, that I had brain damage. When I was little some
doctor said the same thing to my parents, they didn't check it out,
they couldn't' do anything about it anyway.

"You know I believe in God, get on my knees to Him every night".
I was touched by that revelation and thought that surely here he

would appreciate one of mine. "Do _NOT_ INTERRUPT! I can talk to people now, talk to you. And no one can con me, I know when people are not sincere, when they are conning me. And that gets me mad. It gets me upset what the police are doing to me, here on the streets. I'm not going to become an informant, that's what they want. They are messing with my head, planting electronic stuff. And I am not mental! Don't say that I am, this is real. I must have twitched my lips or moved an eyebrow. "DO NOT INTERRUPT!"

"Yesterday walking up this hill these lights on the street, they flickered – messing with my head these cops - and get this…after I took a piss at that mall place, that thing flushed itself, and when I went to wash my hands the thing went on, _by itself!_ They are messing with my head and that gets me upset." I – silly me - felt compelled to explain that lots of things have changed in ten years. "DO _NOT_ INTERRUPT!"

"I wrote a letter to my social worker, it was really long and hard to write. I said a lot of stuff and ended up crying. Did you hear that, me crying . . . I have never done that. What do you think of that?" I remained silent.

"I went down to the police station to tell them to lay off, that I would not be an informant and they are not going to get to me - they didn't pay any attention. I've done a lot of stuff for myself, got these shoes at The Salvation Army, got this coat -$20."

"I used last week, $600 gone on crack. I didn't enjoy any of it. I will never do that again, I will not go back to prison; I will not be homeless much longer and never again. A few nights ago, my bed rocked, they're messing with my head. I sleep on the floor now. It upsets me, having to sleep on the floor . . . but with God how can I lose? God can find me on the floor. What do you think – say something!"

And so...the poor that I have met in shelters do not talk a lot about Elohim. But I sense an overwhelming belief in that presence.

They Call Him Pit-Bull

"I miss my family and East Boston", Pit-Bull told me. "That's home, but I can't be there, my Mom has a restraining order on me; she says I hit my kid sister. I didn't really hit her, I'd never really hit my kid sister" He spoke to his Mom the other night and cried telling her about life in the shelter. She told him to get off the pity pot! It saddened him to hear that his older sister was breaking up with her husband; he said the husband was always good to him, and now his nephew would not have a father. "That makes my stomach upset."

Pit-Bull, size extra large, one of those bodies that are big and solid and not doing anything to make it so, just born that way. Bald, big, round, shiny, shaved head. The people who look -and it is easy to look-, think "tough guy", and so "tough guy" Pit Bull pretends to be. Lots of trouble in the past. Fights - lots of fights - with chairs bouncing off peoples' heads and such - too much jail time. "I'm 32 years old and still doing that crap". Again, his Mother was at that place of NO MORE! She reminded him that many times before when he ended up back at the shelter he had moments of being "a good son", but this time she would wait and hold on to the restraining order. I showed Pit Bull the video on ADHD which leads to Manic Depression in adults; he paid attention as long as he could. "Nice movie" he said, "but Mom is right, I just keep screwing up."

The walking exercise that I recommended was almost complete for the day. Pit-Bull felt better, felt that maybe he even lost a pound. Loud screeches came. Pit- Bull knows every car and every kind of car screech and screeches always get his attention. "Someone's broken down", he said, looking in the direction of the off ramp. Coming closer, he saw that a produce truck was stalled at the top of the ramp. Cars were swerving all over and a small frightened looking man was timidly signaling them away - standing right behind his stalled truck. "Christ he's going to get killed", said Pit-Bull.

A 280 lb Pit-Bull ran - Superman Pit-Bull now in charge! He placed his commanding body further down from the man's small one; far enough down to give the fast approaching vehicles time to avoid a collision. By God, He would make them move over! His body was now transformed back to the disco floors of East Boston -gyrations of every sort: commands, frowns, gestures, Popeye arms flailing up and down. "SLOW IT DOWN! SLOW IT DOWN, GET OVER!, GET OVER!"

In minutes, his mania came into full swing. Commands were interspersed with Attention Deficits: "GET OVER -OVER! . . . nice Jeep Cherokee – dirty rims. GET OVER! . . Honda Accord, Suzuki; *cool* - Mercedes rx7. YOU IDIOT! - SLOW DOWN!, GET OVER! . . Nice Acura 22cl, Chevy prism, Old Town car, nice motorcycle. JESUS WATCH IT!, SLOW DOWN! beautiful tow truck, GET OVER !, GET OVER!". After many minutes of this dance, a State Trooper arrived. While the officer set up flares, realizing that the officer also needed protection, Pit Bull continued his antics of compassion. In his past, how many cops had he run away from, chases on foot and in stolen cars. "Thanks Buddy" said the trooper, "I'll take over now".

No one killed, no one hurt. The small produce man shook Pit-Bull's hand. Pit-Bull grinned from ear to ear of his big, shaved baldhead and returned to the Homeless Shelter to tell the tale.

And so ...perhaps someday as you look upon a street vendor selling hot dogs or fried dough, or way cool cloths, you'll wonder if it's Pit Bull, I hope so.

Street Sacrifice

Stella would seek out all of the King's horses and all the King's men, accept their help, get better and then take just a little crack cocaine - just once more, to ease the pain of life-and fall down again. Her mental illness would reappear, the Children's Services Worker would take another child away, and Stella and her husband Sal would wail as in the time of Herod. They would faithfully visit their children in foster care, then another child born, again a relapse to crack and another child taken and visited faithfully. I am unsure if all the King's horses and all the King's men can put anything together again. I am one of the King's men.

Sal the husband came to me in the streets. "Pappy, my wife she is out of her medication, it is bad when that happens". After making my calls to get information, I told the couple that social workers from the state they had just left were baffled and concerned. They told me: "Stella was doing so well-her longest period of stability-and Sal had just begun an auto mechanic's course; the subsidized apartment took so long to get! The Neighborhood Health Center had just begun to treat them as 'real patients'- they had made friends at the Lighthouse Club. They left it all!" The social worker who did the most work did not even know that the couple had left. "Oh no…" she groaned. "What happened?"

"But pappy", Sal said, "Our oldest, the one they let us keep, they told us that he is in jail in this state. We have come here to be close to him. We have seen him three times and we all cry. Maybe we can find an apartment but we will stay on the street if we have to. We will go back to visit our other children, but Pappy we must be near our son who is in trouble."

I know that the son will be serving a long sentence and over the years will be transferred from one prison to another. And I have no doubt that his Mother and Father will be close by. On the streets, struggling - wailing

And so ...Sacrifices can be found in the streets.

October 31

When I see Bill on the streets, I see his mood. Clearly. When
Bill is spread out under a tree reading a newspaper - I stay away.
Sometimes from a good distance I might give him a soft salute,
he might slightly wave an arm without raising his head. It all has
to do with the bottle, weather he is content or agitated, it all has
to do with the bottle. Recently he told me that he has a problem
with alcohol: "I'm a drunk-that's my problem!", and he tells me
that he's leaving his problem alone for the time being - or for the
forever being...Not hopeful. I honor this, and from time to time
I do no more than sneak in an alcoholics anonymous slogan: -easy
does it -, -one day at a time-, -keep it simple ...buy bonds -, the
last one just to humor him- he has a great sense of humor.

They took the benches out of the park after they fixed it up,
figuring that it is not good to mix the poor with the new
multimillion-dollar civic center across the street. The park looks
nice - and ludicrous with no park benches. The new, improved
and benchless park hasn't kept Bill away, and in time all the others
will come back - they don't need benches, the good earth - ground
zero - is what they are familiar with; benches are actually a hazard -
you fall off them.

On this day it's okay for me to talk to Bill - no newspaper about, no bottle tucked out of view, just sitting on the ground.

\- Hey, Bill.

* Holy shit - excuse my language - I don't want to gross you out but ....do you want to hear what happened to me?

\- How gross?

* Gross!

\- Do I have a choice?

* No.

\- Shoot.

* Christ – excuse my language – I 'm down at the river, the Riverfront, where we go now that they kicked us out of here. And I'm having a beer. Jesus – excuse my language – can't a man have a simple beer without being disturbed like this?

\- Like what?

* Like a hand!

\- A hand?

* One finger missing, half of another, a silver ring in the middle. Raul who is with me drinking the simple beer says: "holy shit Bill, over there, a hand in the leaves! Look!" And yes indeed - holy shit – excuse my language - a hand in the leaves. "What are we going to do with it?" Raul asks me. "What do you mean, 'what are we going to do with it!'   I ain't doing nothing *with it*. What do you do with a hand in the grass for Christ sake – excuse me - missing a finger and a half, with a silver wedding band? "Maybe we should take it to the police" says Raul; Christ - excuse me - a brain the size of a pea. Take it to the police! Like get a bag, wrap it up, toddle on down to our friendly police station..two drunks – and politely drop off a hand, no questions asked?

- Well it's not like you're on the most the wanted list ...but I see your point.
* And I tell this to some of the boys, and can you believe it, one of them says, "So did you take the ring?" Christ – excuse me – can you believe that, did I take the ring! Sweet Jesus, I wouldn't take it off a *live* hand! Do you think that I did the right thing?
- You mean is doing nothing the right thing? And now you tell *me*, thanks a lot! You should probably show me where the hand is.
* Oh no! Oh no!
- Well I can say one thing ...
* What?
- He's probably dead
* Big fucking help you are – excuse me ...
- I just thought of something---today is October 31st!
* So?
-/* H-a-l-l-o-w-e-e-n - TRICK OR TREAT.

We pause, and look at one another.
Bill points. Raul close by is looking at us. We both call out to him, he's moved away quickly. I think I see him smirk.

And so ...At least once a day you will find me walking down the street laughing hard, I'll keep doing the work as long as one day at a time you find me laughing hard.

Reverend Teresa

She was sitting under a large maple tree in front of the Church waiting for the noon day meal; two hundred of those who have no homes will be served quickly this day.

All dressed in white, a small woman, got me to ponder- did not the Buddha reach enlightenment sitting under a beautiful tree? I thought of how she - this Buddha Nature - could represent all of those who sit in the same fashion this day throughout this city, this country, throughout the world-patiently waiting for someone to serve them a meal - "Give us this day our daily bread." Her body was present, she was distant, sending a message that she would not invite you into her space but that she would not shoo you away if you came into it. She was calm and quiet.

Hours before at the day center, I spoke with her for the first time. There too, she was sitting quietly, against the building's wall as if responsible for holding it up. "I have seen you often, you stay to your self, I am Richard, a social worker, may I ask your name?" "Teresa", she answered. "Are you named after the Little Flower, of the Child Jesus, Saint Therese of Lisieux, the Saint of the simple way?" She smiled, a smile that brought forward another person. "Perhaps", she said. -.- - "I believe in simple ways.". She answered my short inquiries directly: yes, this was her first time in a shelter, yes, she is Puerto Rican, no, she did not mind being in the shelter, yes she stayed to herself. She said that she was waiting for a housing voucher and was told that the Governor has put a hold on them, that it could be two years. The wait seemed not to matter to her. Her husband got tired of her she said, "We were married for ten years – he told me to leave, there was no place to go, no one to take me in."

She asked nothing of me. As I left she said softly, "I am a minister of the Pentecostal- God bless you." It is a good way to begin a journey I thought, with the presence of the Buddha, the Little Flower and a Minister of the Pentecostal. "And God Bless you", I answered.

And so   another woman having to cope in the streets because of a male culture. It is hard for me to believe that things have gotten better for women when I often experience this; when I experience this Buddha Woman or this Minister Woman or this Woman of Elohim.

The Monk

There is a place in France on the top of a mountain where men
live a secluded life. Their belief is that if Elohim wills it you will
join them, and if it is meant to be that you are called to leave you
will, and if it is meant to be that you shall return, you shall.
I often saw the man in the soup kitchen and a mental illness. Flat
affect. He always sat alone in this crowded,noisy,turbulent place.
Seemed oblivious to it all. He dressed with care although not
appropriately, for it has been exceptionally hot and he always wore
a sports coat and tie. The meals in front of him were sparse, not
the typical sought-after heapings. He was slim. I thought that he
came from Africa.

In our right season, we got beyond the surface words and talked.
He was from French Liberia. He spoke slowly, sparingly, and
precisely. And he listened. I concluded that the man was a
political refugee and that the depression was from Post Traumatic
Stress Disorder, recalling that many fled Liberia. But weeks later
when we talked directly about mental illness, the man said that he
left his country when he was young, that he went searching about
the world for himself and his God - that he was not a political
refugee. He attributed mental illnesses to possession by the devil-
and that he was not.

Coming back from applying for assistance – he was reluctant to do this - we went to McDonald's. The man would accept only one thin hamburger; he ate it ever so slowly, nurturing in silence each small bite. There would be no conversation until the burger was consumed and it would be a while - a rosary's worth. Silence and precise chewing. When the time came, the man listened intently to each word that I spoke and he smiled broadly when the words turned to faith. "I too, am a Catholic; I get comfort by going to Church. This is not a good shelter, it is dirty and loud and many staff do not care. But the presence of God is within all people - know it, that God is within you and within me. So I can live here. I am tired of looking for a job, I must lower my expectations and look for simpler things, perhaps janitorial - but I do not lose hope, one must never lose hope, for with that you begin to move away from God. I thank you for your help".

The man and I met often and in time, although he did not believe that he was depressed, he allowed me to advocate for a program which gave housing and employment training. But over the weeks of waiting he moved inward as if drawing a cowl over his head. Then he was gone.

There is a place in France on the top of a mountain where men live a secluded life. Their belief is that if Elohim wills it you will join them, and if it is meant to be that you are called to leave you will, and if it is meant to be that you shall return - you shall.

And so… I need to be ever mindful of who I sit across from: The Person, the Monk, the Creator.

૭๑

Not for Nuttin'

"I aint never gonna let anyone hurt you Ritchie, not as long as Gus Leady is around – bottom line, not for nuttin'." I smiled. I like this Gus Leady. A big piece of the work will be assessing the extent of the brain damage caused by the car accident - his friend was killed in that accident. Gus cried when he told me about it, he said that he was the cause, they were both using. I find it amusing to know that someone is out here looking to kill this easy going social worker - good that I have this gangling tough guy, Gus Leady to protect me.

It was hard to get him admitted to inpatient psychiatric care; the gatekeeper was a Dragon Lady. She saw his desire to kill himself as no more than the emotions of a heroin addict – not "true" mental illness, and that it would be a waste of the tax payers' money to have him spend time on a locked ward. After a demeaning assessment, Gus got her permission to go outside of the Emergency Room for a cigarette. Lending support, I told him that he had every reason to be mad and that when the crisis was over we should file a complaint. He said that he knew that she was a bitch but "lots of staff like that in prison Ritchie, you never know what makes them like that, I feel bad for them, I'm extra good to them Ritchie, say "yes sir", "yes ma'am" a lot; makes it easier - Bottom line, not for nuttin'".

As I entered the secured ward, Gus came running down the hall to greet me, looking like the roadrunner, always looking like the roadrunner. "Hey Ritchie! — Hey all you people this is Ritchie who I told you about- my social worker. He's the best, never seen anyone like him, bottom line, not for nuttin'. Stays with me. 'I love ya Ritchie - now what do you think of that - bottom line, not for nuttin'." Over a lot of years I have discouraged people from calling me "Ritchie" - but its o.k. coming from Gus.

Gus told me that he prayed, that he "*really believes*" in God. "Get right down on my knees every night Ritchie and talk. And when you and I begin our talking stuff Ritchie, first we say a prayer-bottom line, not for nuttin'."

Gus is forty-two, since seventeen he has been in prison for all but a few years. A pattern: get out, rob, use dope, get busted, get sick of it all, over-dose to die. He said that he got a call from a friend, "they're planning Ritchie, big job, they want me in. I don't want to do it Ritchie, but this guy is mean - bottom line, not for nuttin'. It will take a miracle to change me Ritchie, I'm forty two and I still depend on, Ma Leady. You'd love her Ritchie; look at these sneakers Ritchie, from Ma Leady, she loves me even though I'm no good. Bottom line, not for nuttin'." In a short prayer we asked for a miracle. I said "Amen", Gus whispered "not for nuttin'."

The plan was that he would stay long enough in in-patient psychiatric care to safely taper off the street Klonopin and dope, followed by a transfer to drug rehabilitation and back onto methadone – our best hope. And from there to *Rosie's Place* to sit tight for six months while waiting for a residential program. I would take the records from the head exam and get him on long-term disability, and in the interim apply for transitional assistance. We had a plan. By the time of his discharge, things were in place, I was thankful that Gus would not have to return to the shelter.

They said that he got out of the cab that transferred him to the drug treatment center, *bounded* into a running car, got behind the wheel and sped off. "All for nuttin'" I thought, "Bottom line, all for nuttin'."

He called me a couple of days later. "Ritchie are you pissed, I know you're pissed Ritchie. Are you going to leave too? I met this lady in the hospital Ritchie, beautiful nice lady; she likes me a lot. She needs me bad Ritchie and I love her, bottom line, not for nuttin'. It's like a miracle how we met Ritchie. Maybe I'll be alright Ritchie, I've taken the methadone, got it here. Maybe I'll be alright. See ya Ritchie, love ya, really love ya, bottom line not for nuttin'"

And so ...Gus, thanks for planting the seed. I have chosen not to come to know the circumstances of your death. Because it does not matter. What matters is that for at least some time, and perhaps up to your death, we had hope. Our journey was "Not for nuttin'."

Not Forever Amber

A Russian Prince courted my mother. He valued the gem Amber and as a Prince, he hoarded the precious stone. My mother's story -in her delusion- continues: "when I turned down his love, he cried tears of Amber and begged that in remembrance of him I name his child Amber." And so I was named. When I was young, I yearned to meet my Mother's scorned Prince; as years passed the tale made less sense to me - and in further time I lost interest. So I am Amber, but recently I think perhaps not forever Amber.

It's been seventeen years since I've seen or talked to my mother. She left when I was twelve. I don't remember why she left, it was sudden. Sadly, I was beginning to forget her. Mostly I remember stories- she would tell me stories all the time. But telling stories in a way different than how teachers read them to me. My mother *believed* her stories! - really believed them. Mother stayed to herself - lived in her own world.

My uncle keeps me informed on Mother's comings and goings, he feels that I care or that I should care. I let him know that I appreciate the updates- sometimes I do, mostly just a little. He called me last week and told me that Mother had lost her apartment- she had lived there for seventeen years - and that she is living in a women's homeless shelter.   He is angry about that, says that this is too much, " the last straw." After he called, I figured that I was suppose to do something, for my mother is now "on the streets"- like a bag lady. But I have not spoken to her in seventeen years!

I ended up talking with a social worker that I liked. The others told me that because of confidentiality they could not tell me anything. But this social worker said that he could, in a general way, let me know how she is doing. He cared about me to. We have had a number of conversations. It was Richard – the social worker - who got me to see what I have avoided - that my mother has a mental illness. He went back and forth on the phone with me - more excited each time - reading me assorted descriptions of possible mental illnesses - like it was no big thing talking about it, wondering about it. On the fourth go around, after listening to the description , I said "that's it, that's Mom." --- "That's Schizoid Personality Disorder, " Richard said . The name bothers me –"schizoid." It has the same ring as "Psycho" - the movie scared me. And it reminds me of skidding – all down hill. My mom who after a delusion named me Amber has "schizoid personality disorder"- Goodness !

I do not know where we go from here, but I sense that this is a beginning place. Richard read to me how treatment is done and what family members might expect. I will never have the Mother that I dreamed of – I too am a dreamer and that worries me - and I do not know if I ever want to see her again.   Richard suggests that we go slowly, that we keep talking.

I know that I can change my name that I do not have to be forever Amber. Maybe it's time but …it's not a bad name.

And so …for every person on the streets and in shelters there are loved ones left back home."Homelessness"trickles back to homes.

Faster than a Speeding Bullet

My name is Superman – it's really David. I don't feel beginnings, middles and ends   don't feel much. Are you wondering if I will be connecting with my family again? -It's been eight years. I left them and went to the streets when I was fourteen. Actually, they left me. They were afraid of me and embarrassed. Even though it's hard for me to get information about the world, I do get it, my psychiatrist and social worker and the homeless nurses are amazed at how much I know. They tested me - I knew most of the Presidents, and about Monica Lewinski and at the end of the exam I remembered the three words given to me to remember: tulip, eye dropper and Abraham Lincoln. By the way, my thoughts run and when I get going I can go on and on mostly because someone is paying attention - that does not happen very much. I have schizophrenia, disorganized type. But I have years of experience of muddling through disorganization, picking up leftovers and danglings. A nice word: danglings. I do that every day, picking up leftovers and danglings.

The voices always come over the radio that I constantly have in my ear- I'm a voice hearer - but I have learned how to over ride them enough to end up getting the news of the world, not that it interests me. Not much interests me. I listened yesterday about how some deaf people choose not to fix their deafness because they believe that being deaf is better than not being deaf. I have been taking this medicine now for three years, a prolixin shot — that's an antipsychotic - every two weeks, and other stuff. They tell me that it makes me better but it feels worse to me because it makes me feel a little. Feeling is not all that good. My social worker tracks me down in different shelters around the country — Massachusetts, New York, Florida - and gets my medicine to me, but this time I may not take it. I want to go back to being Superman. I even had a Superman shirt - I want to shadow box again. Faster than a speeding bullet. I guess to others it was kind of scary when I shadow boxed. I left my social worker a phone message a few weeks ago, I said: "this is me, I just wanted to let you know that I am leaving Harbor House — that's a residential program - and it's for good, for my own personal reasons" (I liked that part "for my own personal reasons") to go to Boston or Worcester. This is a final decision. It's been good working with you, we've had our good times and now I have to go. See you around". I liked that message, classy. Well I went to Florida again, not Boston or Worcester or New York. But like Boston and Worcester and New York, the shelters are so overcrowded that I ended up on the streets - I hate being on the streets. So I called my social worker - I can always get a hold of the people who help me - and I told him that I was just visiting Florida and got stranded, that I did not really want to leave Harbor House for good and that I needed a bus ticket back. I was feeling lousy. My voices were returning, I had been off my medicine for two weeks. So I checked myself into inpatient, I know how to do that, know what to say. I tell them that the voices are telling me to hurt others and myself. It works. Sometimes the voices do tell me that, but not always, but saying so always works. I used to hurt myself, when I was younger, but not in a big way. And I don't like hurting other people. I'll wait here until I get that bus ticket. I was in that Harbor House program for six months, the longest I have been off the streets since I came to the streets seven years ago at age seventeen. It was a good place Harbor House. I took medicine there every day, slept a lot, slept all day for days on end. But my voices told me to move on. They were real profound, they said "move on" Get it, "real profound/move on"? Sometimes I like to kid. I don't always do what the voices tell me, but this time I did. My social worker always tracks me down and gets me back on medication. I'll take them when he tracks me down here - I'm in florida now - but someday I may stop, I don't take them for me. If I stop, I'll end up going back to being Superman, I'll end up swirling with the voices and shadow boxing. Maybe I'll take medicines when he tracks me down because I know its better. But life is swirling when I take them. So either way I swirl, much more than you. I've put on one hundred and twenty five pounds and probably have diabetes, a side effect of the pills. Now I am a very fat superman and I have one heck of a shadow to box. And the last time I met with the doctor, he showed me my shaking tongue and told them that it was a sign that Tardive Dyskincsia was setting in. Aren't you impressed that I know that term – Tardive Dyskinesia - ? I don't know what it is, but it's probably not good. The voices tell me that I am no good and that wanting to talk with my family again after all these years is a stupid idea. The voices say that my family does not want to see me. Let me tell you the truth so that you will not be in suspense any longer. I have met with them. I have met with them already. It happened the last round of in patient hospitalizations, I just told the hospital workers where they were, they called them and my Mom, Dad and Sister came over. And we talked. They invited me out to eat sometime - if I improve my hygiene. They did not say that they wanted to stay in touch with me or anything like that. I don't know what to make of it. I think I have feelings about it - told you feelings are not all that good. It was o.k. to see and talk to them, I never would have done that but for the taking of the pills. We did not hug or anything - I don't hug, sometimes I shake hands, but it's o.k. if people hug me, but no one does. Now that I have told you about this uneventful meeting, perhaps that is where my story ends. You see that is the way things go with me. I don't have a lot of things that build up with great finishes. I just go along. I've got my routines, they are simple and maybe to others, boring. I don't find them boring, just tiring. Got to go. My check comes in today. With all the jumping around that I do, shelters in New York, Florida, Boston, Texas, you would think that I'd miss a check or two, but I don't. I let them know where I am and they send them. I'll buy another cd player, maybe I've had a hundred over the years, I buy them, give them away, buy another. And I'll go out to eat a lot, and maybe get a haircut. See ya.

And so ...I have helped this young man for seven years - he has been all over the country! And he has never missed his prolixin shot ! That pleases me. Two hours ago we hooked up yet again. We took our ride, had an ice cream, he thanked me — three times. And then the ride back - on with the car radio - very loud, pushing lots of buttons. It's eerie ... every time he turns on my car radio he manages to find his favorite song- something to do with "Hey you, Hey you, I'm talking to you" I told him today that every time I hear that song I think of the voices that he hears most of the day, every day, 365 days a year. He smiled, as always, like the Cheshire cat of Alice in Wonderland. Not sure if he heard me.

༄

The Writer

Old tweed overcoat, musty sweater over turtleneck, worn
corduroy pants, short cigar, half glasses, braided hair . . . drinking –
lots of drinking - and homeless. The Writer without a home thinks
himself to be a writer - a Richard Wright, James Baldwin, Fodor
Dostoyevsky, and I know he has the stuff to make it so. I have read
his pieces. And I know that his clock is winding down, that he is
dying in this shelter, it is going on five years now.

"Social worker", he said, "the only thing that I want to do is to
write, and if that doesn't come – the hell with it!" The Writer
served his country in the navy, followed by many short odd jobs -
and there is the drinking. Over the years - many years; one glass
after another, one pint after another, now one quart after another.
He has found comfort thinking that he is not like Ralph in the park
who is up to a gallon a day. I reminded him that there are only
four quarts in a gallon. He came to me recently with drinking
tears and talked of the death of his Mother. How this was a
relationship of crux! To move on I know that The Writer will have
to come to terms with Mom.

I thought that I had come to the perfect intervention: In the
Library, on exhibit in the front hallway, on this "Black History
Week", there was the story of Paul Laurence Dunbar.

Surely, this would inspire The Writer. With him at my side I
pointed directly to the exhibits boldface: "Paul Laurence Dunbar,
the first acclaimed black poet and novelist, writer of 'Lyrics of a
Lonely Life' and several novels, noted for experimenting with the
black voice in literature, died in his mother's home, from TB and
alcoholism." The Writer did not react.

Later that night while sitting across from one another at the soup
kitchen, I added:

* How's the writing going?

- So so - - - look around here, there is so much here to write
about, look at all this pathos.   What are you writing now, no
more crap like last time? (I had read him one of my pieces)

* It's not crap - you're suppose to offer "constructive criticism"-
you're not writing are   you?

- O.K., constructive criticism . . . "nice crap."

* So, enter the contest.

- What contest?

* West County News, Thanksgiving Day issue, theme - "an
anniversary", about 2000 words, by December 3rd, you've got five
weeks- $100 to the winner . . .second and third prizes also. So,
drink and write.

- You enter it - hey why don't you take up drinking, might get
you over the crap.

-* It's not crap; you just don't appreciate my style.

- Stylized crap. Will they take it hand written?

* Yes.

- I don't have any anniversaries; white people with leisure
time have anniversaries...   You mean like fifty years of being
married or five years surviving in this shelter?

* I don't know . . . anniversaries - something that will catch their
interest, something every year, or five years of fifty.

- I don't have anything.
* Make it up Writer, that's what writers do.
- I could make it up....
* Headed again down South soon? It's been five years this week,
right? Long bus ride, all those dirt roads, slow going, time to
think, nothing much to do, quiet, lookout the window and dream
- good time to write huh?
- You mean my Mom's passing anniversary?
* See ya Writer.

And so ...My prayer is that some day you will read this man's works.
Remember that song : I believe:"... I believe that for everyone who goes
astray, someone will come to show the way ..."

My So Called Father

No one is more powerful than 'my so called father.' He has people working for him - he twists their arms. He is criminally insane for sure. He got to that owner at the rest home, got him to switch the room. When I came, they said that I was going to have my own room, but 'my so called father' arm-twisted him - the bastard - and I never got the room. I'm never going back there, but in a while he'll find me again, 'my so called Father', he is really smart but criminally insane for sure.

"My so called father', he tore the blanket, and stole a ten spot out of my wallet; no use in getting anything good, the bastard will just get at it. He is smart; no one can have greater power than 'my so called father'. He left my mother, I was five, went with another woman. I could have been a middleweight, but there was no food in the house.

No use in having more than one set of clothes, 'my so called father', he steals clothes right off your back. He got these clothes on me dirty but I got them clean again. I went into that Laundromat on Wallington Street and asked the lady if I could keep my coat on and take my clothes off. I got those little pieces of soap from the shelter and threw them in the machine. For sure,

I like to listen to baseball but 'my so called father' keeps blurring up the station.

"Three", I never, never, go near that homosexual number that 'my so called father' puts around me. Today at the bank, there were three tellers - he tried to get me to go to one, she kept calling me to come to her. But I let people go around me until another teller came. I never, never go near that homosexual number "three".

Just keep those shoes there, I can't try them on today - Christ, you know that it's Tuesday the third day of the week.

My 'so called father' tries to get me into the water, I never go near water. Who ever told you that dirt is not good for you, dirt just comes off and it does not smell. Garbage smells, not dirt.

The bastard, 'my so called father', wants to be able to find me so he gave me white hair, but I dye it black. That blood on the floor is from being pushed out of the bed by 'my so called father.' What do you mean that he is probably dead by now!, Christ, it doesn't matter how many years pass, 'my so called father', he never dies.

And so …The number 3 with all it's variations: 6, 9, 103 - imagine living with that! And as I smile, imagine helping him! God love him …And me!

Ashamed

Tinh cut off part of his finger "to stop gambling." "No matter bad, good" he said to me, "this is life you have; this is life you need live." Tinh returned to the shelter wrapped in an oversized luminous orange coat on a cold winter's night. "Tinh, where have you been!", I asked. "I so stupid", he said, "in jail, I so, so stupid."

"They told me time up in shelter; I go to camp on river - cold - become so skinny. On streets, meet Quan. Know him back years, know he no good. Quan tell me he know man can give me job. I hungry. Show me man with name Ki. Ki say he have money and want to put in bank, he get me license of business, make me businessman. I open at bank and put money. Later take money out. Do many times- in, out. I think something wrong, that not Ki's money I think. I ask father, mother of Ki- say he o.k. Say belong his money- so bad old people lie you. All time I see Ki, knees shake. He very bad, very smart, have gun, no let me leave. Sleep next to him all time. He not let me out of eyes, I glad when arrest me. Tell all, even Ki license plate number. They catch him no, he run way, he very smart, very smart. I so stupid. How I pay back lots money? I so stupid."

He named all his relatives as if they were next to him; he said that he would remember them forever. He smiled recalling his little sister; she was two when he left Vietnam at seventeen. Now she would be twenty he said and living in Saigon. He told of how his father drank, that he did not work and read lots of books. He told of how the morning before he left, his father poured hot water on him when he was asleep because the father said he was lazy. He said that he left simply because he saw others just get on a boat. He knew it was time to go and that it would be forever. The war was over for three years, how bad the war was. The Viet Cong were in his village and they killed easily. His mother was the last person who he saw and he could tell that she knew he was leaving forever.

They did not speak of it, she gave him a small embroidered pillow. In the beginning and for years he would cry himself to sleep embracing his mother's pillow. In this most recent year, he could cry no more, but he kept the pillow. He landed in Thailand and stayed in a refugee camp for four years. He wrote to his rich uncle in Texas. Chang, the uncle, years before fled Vietnam with his family, not in the middle of night like so many others, but rather by paying a bribe in gold bars. Rich Uncle Chang told him to come to Texas.

After Thailand, Tinh went to a camp in the Philippines. It was there that Chit the Filipina taught him the beginnings of English and of love, but there was no time for nurturing love. From the Philippines to Texas. He stayed for five months with rich Uncle Chang. He said Uncle Chang's wife was mean, that she yelled at him all the time and that it was making him crazy. And school was impossible. His friend one day said that they should go to Ohio – and he left at night; left just as fast as when he left Vietnam. His grandfather who also lived with Uncle Chang, he told his young grandson that he was going to have a hard life, that he would fall down a lot and when he fell down, he should get up again and move on.

For the next seventeen years Tinh went to places: to Shreveport Louisiana, to Columbus Ohio, to Kentucky, Florida, Ohio. He had many jobs, often staying with new found friends, always falling down and getting up again. He learned how to gamble and of a drastic way to stop what became an addiction: cut it off. And now for the past ten years here in this city, staying in shelters and on the streets. Ten years.

Tinh knows that he has a friend in me. He tells me so by singing that fifties tune: "I will follow you". When we walk he always stays behind me,his way of showing deference. Singing in perfect karaoke English: "I will follow you, wherever you lead me." I find it humorous. I slow down. Tinh catches up but quickly falls behind again - "I will follow you, wherever you lead me." I play the game. I zig and zag, stop and go, extend my leg in the air. Tinh zigs and zags, stops and goes, extends his leg in the air. People look. The relationships like Amos to Andy, Abbot to Costello, mostly like Sam to Frodo.

I took Tinh back to the courthouse - the court mandated that he repay a lot of money. I chatted with his Public Defender, she is on Tinh's side, people are always on Tinh's side. We decided that the task would be to get the debt drastically reduced or released but for now Tinh would have to commit to the court that he would pay something monthly from the nothing that he will never get.

We talked of his going back to Texas and Uncle Chang. Tinh shook his head — "no!" Pointing at his clothes, "I never see family looking this". He said that the Chinese value dressing well, that it was a sign of success. "I gone seventeen years, homeless, no good clothes, too ashamed"

And so ... it is not getting better, it seems to have gotten worse, he seems to be forever lost. I accept that more likely than not our journey is over but I stay forever hopeful. It is out of my hands but my door will always be open. P.S. written some time later: The train driver tried to stop, said that he blew and blew the whistle.

Father, is that You?

"Dementia of some sort, a cousin dropped him off a week ago, hard to believe, from Syria to a homeless shelter. He says he's an Aeronautical Engineer, that he speaks four languages and was in charge of some President's plane." Sam, our nurse, gave me the short story. I peeked through the med clinic window – outside on the bench with legs crossed sat an elderly, stately gentleman - a cane with a bone handle comfortably beside him. Sam opened the door and introduced us: "Ishmael, this is the social worker I told you about", and then, "there is something similar about you two!" A breezier than usual introduction from Sam I thought, but yes I did sense a similarity. Not in looks, something in the mannerisms. I thought of my dead father on this the first anniversary of his death; Dad too was an engineer; a well respected industrial engineer - "organize, supervise, deputize and energize" was what I grew up with.

Ishmael paused from flipping pages in assorted small note pads, glanced up at me and then went right back to the page flipping. My father always valued such notepads, he always carried the IBM "THINK" pad in his top suit coat pocket. "Son, if it's important, write it down and have something to write it on." I saw Ishmael's quick glance and knew that I had passed his screening. I knew that

look. I had grown up with it and its flip side: the "disapproval with
no comment" glance.

Ishmael smiled at me, again a facial expression that I knew well. A
smile that said: "Hello, I know that you have your story too - we all
do - but I am not interested, there is no time, I am thinking about
more important matters, about my situations." My father thought
like that, always charting his courses, going his way, dealing with
his situations. My father dressed well; Ishmael, homeless in a
shelter, dresses well. Clothes hang right, accoutrements- pocket
watch, tie pendant, cuff links - are discrete. Smells are not
overbearing. A ring is worn. Sport coat of fine fiber, four buttons
on the sleeves, my father made jest of men who wore the common
three. While we talked, Ishmael took out a lighter and singed the
end of his tie, something that came to him with ease - there would
be no loose threads about him. There were no loose threads about
my Dad. I noticed Ishmael's well kept finger nails, like my father's
- another of the select who take inordinate care of dead cells.

"Now, you must take me back to see that bastard second cousin
of mine Omar." We had just met and I was being told what to do.
There would be no deference to a social worker. My father went
about his tasks that way - directly, and he always, always had tasks.
"But before we visit idiot second cousin Omar we will have our
picture taken". Ishmael thrusts a camera into the hands of another
shelter guest; the shelter guest just did it with no questions asked.
A picture was taken. We are now smiling for the camera, like on
a holiday. Ishmael said, "I always take pictures and I have many
albums, with the names underneath so I can remember." My
father would say, "do not forget names son, it is important to
remember names."

At Omar's house, we sat in the shade in the back yard and had Turkish coffee. I asked questions of bastard, idiot, second cousin, collecting information so that I could understand Ishmael's predicament. I did not find second cousin an idiot, but rather pleasant. We talked about Ishmael as if he were not there; he said nothing and seemed disinterested. In his final years when my father was in trouble with the family because of his drinking, a "family meeting" was convened (an efficient management tool "the family meeting", put into place by father and now seemingly turned against him.) This was a family meeting with a twist, Father did not know it was coming, an "alcoholic intervention" with a therapist facilitating. Father said nothing, just took notes. The therapist said that in all his years he had never met anyone who was both so intently loved and disliked.

Urgency surrounded Ishmael - urgency always surrounded my father. Now for Ishmael there were matters to get to...lawyers to be contacted - about the green card and an accident settlement; a follow up hernia surgery appointment, letters to be written, people in assorted countries to telephone, an apartment to clean out, and a service at the mosque to attend, relatives to find. Dutifully I kept up, as I always did for my father.

I hoodwinked Ishmael into seeing a specialist in dementia, a Neurologist from Lebanon. He did not like the questions asked of him, "This doctor is for people 'crazy in the head. and he is from Lebanon!". Ishmael announced to the whole clinic and to the world that he was leaving - leaving period. He left with assorted medical personnel running after him - "but, but Ishmael ... "I smiled recalling how my father marched out of hospitals.

The Airline Attendant politely said to Ishmael that he could not go into the clearly closed off section. Ishmael roared - in English and Arabic, with references in both to the inferiority of black people. In my father's world there were people deemed of lower station and being curt to them was permissible. Security came running. It was nothing short of a miracle my convincing them that this was Ishmael's mental illness speaking and that all in all he would be fine on his journey home to Syria. I was not convinced of that. My sigh of relief was loud as Ishmael left my sight to board. I trusted that the Travelers Aid people who I spoke with would connect with him at his layover in the Netherlands and that there would be no trouble on the plane. Relieved, I left it in the hands of Elohim.

As the plane took off for some reason I recalled that shortly before his death I got a call from my father, "Richard there are ocelots on my ceiling, big ones . . .this is not good,be well son, do good works, I'll come and visit from time to time."

And so. . .We have our images of who are the "homeless", there are so many exceptions that it is best that we conclude: "There but for the grace of Elohim go you or I"

Happy South of the Border

* Blaire – let's get out of here, the snow's coming down fast.

- That bitch, she wouldn't cash my check, I ain't leaving.

* Blaire, this is the Bank of America, United States, a *bank* - lots of suits and they're all staring.

- (With a booming voice mixed with experienced crying) That bitch behind the counter wouldn't cash my check. She said I need identification ; I told her that I'm homeless for Christ sake, that I slept in an abandoned building last night and got raped and that I need the money to get fucking identification so that I *can* get a room somewhere - and if no one cashes my fucking check I ain't going anywhere.

* (Diversionary tactic # 1) Sure is a big bag.

- All my stuff, living on the streets, getting raped, that bitch, she wouldn't cash my check!

* The cops are coming.

- I don't care, well - I'll tell them that this bitch wouldn't cash my fucking check.

* Shit, stop swearing, we'll get it cashed at Grahams.

- No we wouldn't, I tried that already.

* How about that place next to the recycling center?

- No! - Can't – damn it, tried there, *you'll* just have to cash it.

* Yeah right, I don't carry money, wife's orders.

- Smart wife. Well then tell that stupid bitch to cash the fucking check!

* Right, yell out "hey stupid bitch cash the fucking check." How did you get that bag in here? (Diversionary tactic # 2)

- Dragged it – must weigh 50 lbs and with me 300- over 300 - that's a lot. From Mason Square, two buses, all the way down Main, in this cold and snow. Look at all the stuff falling out! Went through Jackson Square. . . I always wanted to live in Jackson Square, in that tan building off Sherman Street; but they wouldn't take me because I've been in jail and I always wanted to live there as an adult after growing up there as a kid - over at the study home. . . I belong in that neighborhood; no I *belong* in that neighborhood! I went to the study home there from 61 to 66 - with my mentor teacher Mr. Pond. And his mother was the Housemother and my female mentor. And her husband used to make homemade root beer soda and root beer barrels – damn, I can't see without my glasses! My mom says she wouldn't let me go back to her house by myself to get my diabetic kit and my glasses, she wants *you* to come with me, because Calmer Green is going to evict my mom if I come there by myself, even to get money and my glasses and my diabetic kit - now isn't that something! That's why I haven't had them for a whole week, because I was rushing to get out when mom kicked me out and I forgot them on the kitchen table – maybe tomorrow we could try to go to my mom's and get them? I need'm bad.

* I'm not going to be around tomorrow.

- Where are you going to be?

* I 'm going to be at a statewide meeting.

- What statewide medium?

* *Meeting,* just a meeting

- I would like to go to one of those state wide mediums because I am a peer advocate for consumers
* It's not that kind of a thing
- What is it?
* It's a – it's a staff meeting, not going to be any mediums there - well maybe one or two
- That's what you're going to! Hey they would be glad if a consumer came, I know for a fact because I went to several staff mediums with social workers under the mental health in the 90's and the head Director was glad that a consumer came along
* (Diversionary tactic # 3) Pretty sunset over there
- Excuse me?
* Pretty sunset over there.
- They always are around here. Jesus they got to cash my check!
* Speaking of Jesus, you sort of look like Santa Claus, but you're scaring people.
- Reminds me when I met Coretta Scott, she said I looked like a Christmas Angel. A *Christmas Angel*! The first time was at Ebenezer Baptist Church, second time after Martin got shot. Coretta Scott said: "Blaire, you haven't changed a bit, still have that angel puffy face, and those curls.
* You chatted with Coretta Scott King!
- I lived at the study home on Sherman street from 61 to 65, met them on Easter Sunday 63, talked to them both and then not again till 83 when we went for the Anniversary March.
* (Back on track tactic) You could file a complaint, let's get out of here, file a complaint tomorrow.
 - I want my damn check cashed.
* I think we have about a minute before the fat lady dances.
- What does that mean?
* It means cops are coming to arrest us — correction *you*.

- Well, I 'm the fat lady – now weigh over 300 pounds- close to
400 - and I isn't dancing and I know all the cops, drive me crazy.
Cops. The time of the fire we had stayed at my mother-
in- law's and went straight from her house in South Boston to our
supportive work shops on Plantation Street - so it wasn't us. Back
in 76, on May 26 - so it will make 30 years ago that I got set up
for a crime that I didn't even do - set up by a bad cop and a rich
landlord Jew named Wackawitz. His money talked so much that
the Judge sat there a whole year waiting to decide and then sent
us to jail. And in 77 cops shot at us in front of City Hall one night.
I was able to duck into the bushes. When you got cerebral palsy
you can't duck in the bushes so my husband Harry took a bullet
unarmed in the back by a coward cop. And you want to know
why he's a coward – because soon after that he dropped dead of a
heart attack chasing a suspect. See, as my Pastor said - my Pastor
said if you mess with God's children you're a coward and you get
fifty strikes. You know disabled people put up with a lot. They can
put up with more pain and disappointment than a normal person
- isn't that something, that you could not put up with the pain
or the disappointments that I have put up with for thirty years ?
That's why Pastor said that I am a child of God 'cause I put up with
so much. Thirteen times in my life time I should have been dead.
The first time was when I ate the arsenic and honey put out for
the rats and the last time was the day after New Years outside the
Salvation Army on Appleton street in Holyoke when a drunk drove
right up on the sidewalk and knocked me right through the glass
door. There was this little tiny Puerto Rican man standing there
- I landed on top of him and the guy couldn't have weighed more
than 120 pounds. But when he was on the street, he was lusting
at a female across the street that looked good and he got happy
south of the border and when I landed on him I deflated him and

he thinks that I did it for six months because when he found out that I weighed 300 pounds, plus he was begging for mercy, for the cops to get me off of him but they wouldn't move me until the ambulance got there and that poor little guy was begging for mercy- in Spanish and English. ... I'm hungry, let's get out of here, I'll get you a cheese cake across the street at Paul and Elizabeth's – best cheese cake in town – really, everything kosher - but I'm Evangelical.

* Thought you didn't have any money?

- I lied.

And so . . . we lumbered across the street – it took two turns of the light – me carrying all the stuff, Blaire chattering away about cops, the check not cashed, cheesecake and deflations. At Paul and Elizabeth's they shooed us to the back almost before we entered the store! The cheese cake was good; the coffee great, snow was lightly falling. The company alive and the day almost over. I need Tango tonight!

Pore Judd is Daid

(*From the musical Oklahoma)

-So you've done gone and done it – you're dead!

*As a doornail, *my little chickadee.*

-What happened?

*I bought the farm, bit the dust, yodeled the last yodel.

-Yodeled the last yodel?

*Officially, a heart attack - never knew I had heart problems …
never knew I had a heart. I read before I *departed* that fear can do that
to you. *Maybe I was a fearing.* But it was mostly the other thing.

-I know - the other thing. When they told me, right away I began
to sing *Pore Judd is Daid,* it just was there. I sang it just like them,
real slow and emotional like:

"Poor Judd is daid
poor Judd Fry is daid
all gather round his coffin now and cry
he had a heart of gold and he wasn't very old
 oh why did such a fella have to die ?"

What do you think of that?

*Pathetic.

-I knew that you'd like it.

*I was glad to move on, it was time – everything has its season.
A time to live, a time to die - sometimes we're happy, sometimes

65

we're sad, some times we laugh, some times we cry…Sometimes we throw up!

-I'll miss our soup kitchen therapy sessions.

*They were therapy?

-Yeah, I knew the only way that I could get anywhere with you would be by keeping it humorous, you would have run away from typical stuff.

*More like you couldn't find a couch in the soup kitchen.

-So did it help?

*What?

-The therapy !

*Not that much, I'm dead, remember. Well I guess so, I felt better afterwards. What did you learn about me?

-Nothing until the end when it was too late - except that you were likable. But even though we were not getting anywhere particular we were going someplace real good. I now call it "Presence Therapy"

*"Presence Therapy"- Snappy!

-In the beginning I was sure it was the drink – what is the most likely thing to bring a Certified Public Accountant to the streets I asked…got to be hitting bottom.

*Which is why you asked me if I knew Bill W? I had no idea who the hell you were talking about - know him now, founder of Alcoholics Anonymous – (sung) *he's dead too.*

-So not the best place to take a job – considering.

*You mean at the *sanitary landfill*?

-Yeah the dump

*They offered me a job - I was homeless remember - it helped me forget the room issue.

-That room must have been a hoot.

*Health Inspector called it *Oh my God!*

-So how long did you have it.

*The hoarding?

-Yah the hoarding.

*Long time. Got so that I couldn't move, in my room and in my head. Totally consuming, knew it was nuts, but could not stop or tell anyone, too embarrassing. Ate me up. Imagine it, a CPA / Hoarder. It was killing me, so I moved on, good to be rid of the clutter. See you - and thanks - and don't take any wooden nickels

Do you know the second verse?

"Poor Judd is daid
a candle lights my head
I'm lookin oh so purty and so nice
I looks like I'm asleep
it's a shame that I woun't keep
but it's summer and they're running out of ice."

And so… my folks die earlier, but I am always surprised when it happens.

The Empathic Potato

I found Itzak Pearlman, the famous violinist, in the soup kitchen today. I wasn't surprised to see Itzak Pearlman in the soup kitchen today, just delighted that I found him among that sea of people. Darleen, the manager told me that she has never seen it that packed. Itzak Pearlman thinks that he is Itzak Pearlman. I think that he is probably not and that he and I are in for a ride-schizophrenia does that to folks.

I maneuvered my way over to the far end of the soup kitchen where he sat. We "chatted", neither of us understanding anything that the other said. I ended it abruptly for Itzak was getting to "a place", and I knew that the soup kitchen staff did not want him to get to "a place" again so soon after being banned for three days. I maneuvered back across the hall and was about to leave when I heard - we all heard - a loud "SOCIAL WORKER, GOOD BYE!" I turned around just in time to catch a glimpse of an airborne thing headed for *my* head. Instantly and with nonchalance, I raised my right arm and plucked the potato out of mid air. Caught the spud in mid air! In social work there is nothing more important than establishing the "empathic bond" Sometimes the "empathic bond" comes by catching an Idaho potato.

And so ... I told Itzak that I had never seen his Synagogue; he said "lets go" and there we were. On that day in their temple hall they were exhibiting the Holocaust. I felt that I was on sacred ground - the Catholic social worker given a tour of the Holocaust by a Jew with untreated schizophrenia - The event transcended the labels and gave personal meaning to each.

Symphony Hall Gentleman

Police don't beg. The record breaking snow was over, now it was a record breaking minus 47 degrees at 2 A.M. in Court Square. "Friend, let us take you to the shelter". They offered three times and then left him at his "bed" on the top step of Symphony Hall stairs. He knew his body, knew that he was far beyond "under the influence" and all the other cute expressions that did not capture his loneliness. He knew that he would have to be careful, knew that he was starting not to feel the cold and that was bad. He had never peed on himself and no matter how cold, he would not now. So he left his cardboard box bed and pile of blankets, walked to the ledge, fell over and hit his head.

When he came to, he inched himself to a seated position. He knew he could not get back to the cold warmth of his cardboard bed, and now he could not feel his feet – a very bad thing. He looked up at the hanging posters from Symphony Hall: *Kiss Me Kate, Coming Soon.* "Not to me" were his last material words. His buddy found him a few hours later and cried.

The buddy found him still and stiff with one foot exposed. They had a memorial service for him on the site, at Symphony Hall, where the two of them slept, one a step below the other. Two vets, buddies, who drank to forget and remembered to share. All said of the dead man that it was a shame, that he was a gentleman, that he never caused harm, that because he was so drunk on that bitter cold night no one should have sold him anymore and where were the cops.

The veterans from the streets came to the memorial, for one of their own. They stood at attention, in uniform or parts thereof. Short, tall, thin, mustachioed, bald, fat - at attention, saluting. At the end of the line, somber and politely not- so-sober, the buddy, saluted with his arm raised a quarter of the way, the best that he could do. Ragged, tired, layered, weathered face and swollen hands, at attention, saluting, saying good bye.

The night after the death the buddy and I talked. Again it was a record frigid night. We talked on a park bench, in Court Square across from Symphony Hall. In the dark, two bumps on a log. The buddy was pleased that he had not yet started the pint for the night, that he was able to still sit straight, still talk straight, in Court Square, in the dark, in remembrance - this was a time to be less then totally drunk.

"I was shot twice, stabbed twice, in Vietnam and the Gulf War-one lung left", he said without boast or pride. "I was a soldier, trained to be in the cold", and after a pause, "they have been trying to get me to go into that shelter, I will never go into that shelter – they robbed me, they are violent." "I am sad" he continued, "my son and his wife no longer let me see my grandchild and I am sad that I cannot put away my drinking. And my friend is dead". Softly on the bench in the middle of the park in the dark he said to me: "I am not scared of the cold, but I am scared of returning to where we slept."

Disheartened and about to leave, I remembered that just for this cold spell the Rescue Mission Shelter -a different shelter- opened its doors. There it was clean and safe. I drove him there. In he went. On at least that night, this gentleman would be warm, a warmth that would allow him perhaps to dream. Probably not a good dream, but a dream nonetheless.

And so ...most "drunks" that I know will share the bottle; not only that, they know where each other's tolerances are and will sacrifice "theirs" to meet the needs of the sicker. Does that not say something good about the human condition!

The Looking Glass

"Dan I'm not telling you this to make you feel guilty, it wasn't you."

"Yesterday I came down the stairs in our home, on my way to the breakfast table. In the mud room I saw my wife on the phone, an unusual time for her to be on the phone. She was serious, and pale. I could hear our daughter on the other end, she was crying. My wife handed me the phone. I knew something was wrong and it was serious. I stop here to tell you that our daughter and four and a half year old grandchild are o.k. You may not remember any of this, because you are drunk; I repeat - our daughter and grandchild are o.k. Physically- emotionally it will take time.

"They were driving on 91 in the passing lane going 65 miles per hour. Out of nowhere a car sideswiped them in an attempt to pass through an impossible space. Bad judgment. Our daughter's car went out of control, mother and daughter were screaming as the car went all over the highway. The spinning stopped when she hit a car head on.   But for the grace of Elohim they are alive and by their guardian angels o.k.

"A policewoman was immediately on the scene; she told our daughter that she saw the car that caused the accident, and that, 'it was all over the road, a drunk driver'. She said that she was about to pursue the drunk driver when the accident happened, instead she chose to assist the victims"

Through his stupor Dan winced, a wince of compassion, he lowered and buried his head on the table. And I left hoping that this served a purpose.

And so ... with my family history it's a struggle for me to help alcoholics-perhaps I end up doing it because of that history.

A Woman of Dignity and Strength

She always notices me as I approach her perch, the large flower pot on Main Street. Our approaching eye contact told me that I would be allowed to stay a bit. The drink not totally smothering her yet. She pointed at her head with both hands, her gesture of approval of my choice of the hat for the day. Sitting down next to her – now two human beings in a flower pot - I wrote down the affirmation: "Just For Today I am a Woman of Dignity and Strength."

Looking into my eyes and soul she slurred her predictable: "He left me again Clem (my name is Richard, but I now like it when she calls me Clem), he went with her to get dope. Oh Clem, it hurts so much!" I put my fingers to my lips motioning for her to be still and handed her the affirmation: "Just For Today I am a Woman of Dignity and Strength." She read it, slowly and again, and tears fell. The mascara of the streets ran. She lowered her head, shook it to the right and left. .She extended her hands, I took them. A most human moment.

And then: "Go Clem, you gotta go Clem, I gotta work" – "Ma'am, spare change, can you spare some change ma'am?"

And so ... the spirit that this woman has in spite of it all! Textbooks have been written about women who stay in abusive relationships; we are still trying to understand it. I am still trying to find the right "intervention" for her. But again it is being present that gives me joy and brings a smile to her face. And therein we both find comfort in something much bigger than us.

That Stupid Ass Hat!

It did not bother me that whenever I came close to her she scowled and took off muttering. I knew what the muttering meant: "Stupid ass social worker, psycho babble, pill this, pill that - screw you" I say "not bothered" because I expect just about anything from the streets. What works is riding it out, holding my ground, patience, easy does it stuff. *Usually not bothered.*

On this day at the soup kitchen, for the first time she spoke to me, yelled at me: "WHY DO YOU WEAR THAT STUPID ASS HAT!" "Stupid ass hat!" I was stunned! I like this damn hat - everyone likes this damm hat! I had seconds to respond or let it go. The appropriate answer should have been something like: "lots of times people who I help need to find me quickly so it helps." She came close to me - never this close before - and I said in a whisper: "because I have face cancer and next week my whole fucking face is going to drop to the ground and in front of *YOU*." And I stuck my tongue out at her. Not professional- but a good feeling. More often, we now talk. I may tell her that I lied about the cancer and maybe, just maybe I'll acknowledge that perhaps the hat is ... no, no, a thousands times no, I'll stand up for the hat!

And so ... totally real really helps on the streets.

Victoria of Victoria House

From the top of the Victorian staircase she looked down at me:
"Yes, if you want to come again just call me here - and thanks."

I met her the week before. Our journey came to its end when I
got her into this Victorian rooming house run by nice people. A
place perfect for her. She likes it; - a lot- and she appreciated my
showing it to her. I am touched by her; by her beauty, grace and
charm. Beauty, grace, and charm in spite of living on the streets.

To your misfortune you would not have noticed her on the park
bench; she is skilled at going unnoticed. She would be tired, so
her head would be down just enough not to cause you to wonder.
She is very clean. A small woman, wheeling a small duffle bag and
another small carrying bag. She points to the duffle bag, "look
what I got for two dollars at the dollar store!" No bag lady here.
The packing is masterful. "I keep the daily things in this small bag,
its fits nicely on top of my new two dollar bag which I can push."

In the beginning she did not engage with me, did not engage
in a manner that said: "I was taught not to talk with strangers".
But when I gently pursued as I am called to do, she forgot the
childhood warning. She wanted to talk to another person, and in
no time she talked on and on. But not the on and on that makes

no sense, not the on and on that begs to be stopped, not the
on and on of mania. I was surprised that so many words could
continue to flow with sense. If I did not cut it off, could this on
and on that made such sense never end? Perhaps it would after the
telling of the stories of years and years of isolation, years and years
of no one to listen. Now in her Victorian place there would be
listeners - this pleased me.

"It is my birthday so I got myself these; how much do you think
they cost? This one was $1.50. And this blouse - $ 1.00. Glad
that I wouldn't have to stay at that shelter, they do not allow you
to take a shower in private; I need to take a shower in private,
I cannot take a shower with another person near me - is that
unreasonable?

"My sister, she did not give me the money that I deserved, I could
not complete my schooling. I was interested in languages -
because I was the one that had to take care of my father when he
got sick. I came right home after my job in the bank and took
care of him. The promise was that I would get paid, but I didn't.
And then when he died it was supposed to be that I would always
have a place to stay, but they said that was only for as long as they
were not selling the house and my sister said that they were selling
the house and that I would have to find some place to live. I
complained to some of my cousins, but they did nothing. She was
not going to really sell the house, she just wanted me out. I said,
"then you will have to evict me", and she did evict me.

"So I went to California. I went there once when I was a kid, to
visit an aunt, and I liked it; so I went there, to find her, but I could
not, she was not there, so I found an apartment and I stayed in it

for three years, but they sold it and I could not afford anything - the apartments cost too much; so I stayed on the streets, except sometimes I would stay a few days in a hotel. This policeman began to bother me. He said that if I did not move on he would arrest me and I was doing nothing wrong, just nodding with my head down a little, not sleeping on a bench, I would never sleep on a bench, how could I watch my things if I were sleeping on a bench. I know how to nap sitting up, nap so I am still awake. And then I decided that I should go back to where I grew up, so here I am. I don't believe in mental health; I had a friend that went into the hospital and she said that they never let her go. This place . . . they will not keep me will they? My father drank a lot, it was amazing that he never lost his job, and when he drank he was not nice, he was very hard to get along with. This is a nice enough room, I can make it good, I will get some fabric."

I have not seen Victoria since I got her into Victoria House a year ago. Time for us to "do tea".

And so . . . I have a tendency not to "do tea" with folks who have moved on, because there are many others who await our beginning My hope and trust is that others like you will follow, to continue the journey.

You Go Kid

He said he was 18. In the shelter no one believed him. I did. The kid beamed when he told me he was no longer under DSS – the agency for abandoned kids, they're always out of there at eighteen, on the same day, gone; kids now with a big title :"emancipated minor" - another way of saying; "you're on your own kid!" We went for an interview for Job Corps. To my surprise the kid was there waiting for me, on time and looking bored. And with GREEN hair! When I did my #17 preparing for the interview speech, it did not occur to me to say, "And don't dye your hair green"!

The Job Corps representative kept us waiting. This concerned me for the delay brought the kid between two chairs into a napping position worthy of a Chinese gymnast. How come he doesn't fall - must be the same principle that keeps those pants from just never quite falling down. Time to wake him up. I lifted one ear piece: "earth to planet green hair . . . get up!"

"Wasn't asleep, never am." "You lie", I joked. I was struck how this little man with dyed green hair - now lip synching an incredibly nasty song - could come back to the real world so quickly. Out of context he uttered not looking for an answer, "So how did I deserve this life?" I felt that I could tell him. I quietly sang it from West Side Story: "Officer Krumpky he's done it again, this boy don't need a shrink he needs a year in the pen - but officer Krumpky, he's depraved because he's deprived." "You're depraved because you're deprived." The kid got it – I think.

A diamond in the rough this kid, I pray that he will land on his feet in this tough world. I knew that my time being the Dad or Big Brother was up, just a speck of sand on the beach of this relationship. I gave him the street kid reality speech: "even though you have been dealt a raw deal, it's up to you to make it and you can. There will always be someone around to help, but in the end it will be you and you alone. Sorry to have to break this to you. And there are two paths, you know what they are.

Job Corps accepted him on condition that he get rid of the green hair. "No problem", he said, "I've always wanted to be bald." His first choice was masonry, his second college prep. In the elevator I was startled by the kid's reaction, a total attitude change - "Yes!" with the pulling down of the arm thing. We got ice cream cones and ate them while dangling our legs from the tail gate of my truck. He with his nasty music and green hair, me with my lovely tango tunes and white hair. And we're thankful for a beautiful spring day.

And so …it has been a long while since I've heard how he's doing, yesterday I believe that I saw him on the streets, in a different place, a place of more opportunity . I was sure that it was him for there is something about his gait – a confidence -   even from the back and from a distance. And from what I saw, it looked good. You go kid!

༄

Next In Line Please

Cecelia – her name plate reads – a woman who does not notice
that a lot of heads turn her way - a striking woman. Her body
is that nice, her clothes colorful, her black shoulder length hair
styled. Enough of that, for it is her way that defines her. She types
fast while never lowering her eyes away from you. She listens
captivated! At spots she will ever so slightly tilt her head at an
angle that says: "that is interesting!" She will lightly puff up her
cheeks then hollow them out while puckering her lips - charming
habit. Her eyes wide open one moment speaking a disbelieving -
N-o-o! and then to a squinting painful- Oh No ! And always her
head slightly rocking up and down saying - I understand, please go
on. All the while typing, always typing. A woman who takes care
of herself, of her things, of those who she loves. Her desk without
clutter, her jewelry simple -expensive and not excessive- a photo
close by, in a gold frame, of her family: a muscular handsome
husband, two beautiful children – one boy one girl; a white
picket fence around a ranch house. A woman in control and not
controlling. Hispanic.

The "applicant"-my charge- appreciated having such a listener,
for it had been a long time since anyone listened to her. A short
woman with common features, a woman with all her belongings
stuffed into a worn, dirty duffle bag. A woman with no relatives or

friends, a woman oblivious to the needs of others - who takes her teeth out before she speaks – for they hurt - spits them in her hand with no qualms and pockets them. A woman who had no time to bathe today, and yesterday and perhaps the day before that - a woman who now eagerly goes on and on, as intent to talk as the other is to listen.

"I got out yesterday, Framingham–that's for women. I wrapped, did 11 years. I'm legally blind, from the diabetes. Didn't kill Raymond, if I wanted to kill him I wouldn't have poisoned him, I would hit him over the head with a hammer. The witnesses lied."

"You know this woman came up to me in the women's shelter last night, she said, 'the next time you want my lover to do something you ask me first – no one hits on my old lady'. I showed her my fists and told her that I wasn't hitting on anyone but I know the best place to hit is at the neck and I just got out for murder - that shut her up".

"Christ they let me out with some medicine that I've never used before and it spoiled - $3,000.00 worth- cause it was supposed to be refrigerated. And they left my syringes in the van, so I have my insulin and no way to get it in me! And as I am talking to you now I am way overdue for a shot. I haven't eaten and I need to get to a hospital! They drop me off in this fucking city and no one knows what to do".

And the interview proceeds, one ranting, one listening.. After it ran its course, the interviewer thanked her, walked her to the waiting area, said "good luck" and meant it. "Next in line please."

And so…It bears repeating – from <u>Snow falling on Snow</u> by Robert Wicks: *"Presence is truly one of the best gifts we can offer to others in need. The value of presence to another person should not be understated. When we sit with people in the darkness and 'help them cry' we model hope and new possibilities in ways even we sometimes don't realize."*

From Embalming Fluid to Soup du Jour

I was sitting next to Angel at the soup kitchen when the now so
cool Alvaro graced us with a visit. I moved Alvaro on from the
homeless shelter several months ago. Seeing his friend, Angel
beamed approval. Now when Alvaro visits, everything matches -
the socks, the sunglasses, the watch, the shoes. Alvaro is new,
Alvaro is hip. See the new, hip Alvaro. On this overcast day when
Alvaro graced us with his visit to this dank kitchen, everything
about him was sky blue - sky blue silky sweat suit, sky blue
baseball cap, sky blue watch, sky blue sneakers and a big sky blue
ring which in cursive screamed:"*ALVARO!*"

As I went around the corner of the soup kitchen line I leaned into
Alvaro's space and extended a piece of paper-"autograph, may I
have your autograph, sir?" He smiled. Alvaro and I know each
other well; I've helped him a lot over this year. He paid me no
mind and called out to a man nearby: "Amigo, como esta? The
man did not answer, Alvaro called out again - and again. Finally,
"Alvaro! – is that you?" Alvaro smiled., he has a devilish smile.

There was no smile when I met him last year; there was nothing
on his face. We call it "flat affect." Day after day in the Day
Center he would sit. Quietly - not reading, not talking to anyone,
not watching TV, not sleeping - just sitting, sitting. I know this

stillness; it is unsettling to feel it. When I feel it I fast forward and remember what a gifted social work teacher said to me: "you have great instincts but you need to be more direct"– I've been direct with Alvaro.

Alvaro came home one afternoon when he was twelve and saw his father leaning over a dead person, a smoking gun in his hand. He told me that his father got a life sentence with no chance for parole - and that's all that he told me. Nothing said about the dead person and about the testimony that Alvaro surely had to give. One more thing - he said that he hated his father and missed his mother.

Maybe he'll tell you more – Alvaro, say Hello.

"Hello; why do I do what this social worker tells me to? I never drank, never did street drugs; after the killing, I went to selling. Fuck it! It was embalming fluid that I sold – not drugs – the fluid's used to make angel dust. I sold embalming fluid cause I don't like being around real drugs. The year in prison was scary. I didn't talk to anyone. And when it was over, I couldn't go back, so I got on a bus and came to the only other city that I know, and to this shelter. Never been in a shelter. It's very dirty and very bad."

"I have diabetes, found that out in prison – serious diabetes. The nurses here told me that I could die. I paid them no mind, just sat in the day center — day in and day out and kept to myself. I saw Richard - this social worker, often he comes to the Day Center – I find watching people interesting. One day he comes over and says, "Hey friend, plan on dying? - Nurses say you're not taking care of yourself. "No introduction, no chit chat, just that I'm going to die!"

"Which surprised me - not that I was going to die, that was the idea - it surprised me that I guess he cared. And weeks later there I am taking his suggestion, talking with a psychiatrist and taking medication for depression. Richard told me that in addition to popping off soon - from not caring for my diabetes -, that I was depressed, *real* depressed. With the medication my depression is less, I can tell. But I did nothing about the diabetes. I ate all kind of sweets; it's easy to get sweets here, you nice people all the time bring over cakes, cookies and other junk. Richard got me away from the shelter and into a home for folks who he said, 'are really messed up ' 'Thanks a lot, I said'. He drove me to this better place which is where I am now. A house with only five other nutty people and nutty staff: And a nurse, some rules, my own room and no rent. Not bad, it helps. A much better place but I still wasn't caring for my diabetes, wouldn't take the insulin, still ate sweets, wouldn't go to the specialist. So Richard comes over and says: 'You take care of you self and I'll get you six hundred dollars a month.' I had no idea what he was talking about but it got my attention. He told me about social security disability, said that he'd get me on it, but only if I were alive. Ha Ha!"

"Now I get $ 600 a month and that explains my hats, my watches, my matching outfits- tomorrow everything will be pink! Richard says that soon this will get old and then he tells me something that I guess I knew: 'You are smart, selling embalming fluid was stupid but on the smarter side of stupid.' He says that it's time to move the ship out of the harbor – something about dry rot - and go to cooking school. Just like that: 'go to cooking school'. And he plopped down a community college catalogue."

"From selling embalming fluid to stirring soups – I guess that I'm going to cooking school."

And so ... One person can make a difference.

Thank you

Thank you! His Thank always higher than his you. Throughout the day the same simple sincere musical Thank you! When anyone is drawn to try to talk with Hiep Trong they are taken aback and delighted at his ending all of their words with his Thank you! I am with Hiep often these days and always touched by his "Thank you's . . .and compelled to answer with my mirrored, "You're welcome!" Hiep acts gratefully in spite of it all: Vietnam solider boy, jungle fighting, killing, gunshot to the head, napalm, family dead. He keeps it to himself. And then being scooped up from the embassy rooftop minutes before the fall of Saigon, dropped off to the land of opportunity, losing his papers within a month and wandering the streets - now for 29 years. Twenty-nine years!

I have experienced it several times; a person speaking to Hiep will stop in mid sentence and say . . ."I like you!" Thank you! I too have liked a person upon a first meeting but have never told them so then and there. Hiep brings out the best in people. Some tell him why they like him: "you have a kind face", "you look like Buddha", "you move peacefully." He does move deliberately - having lost all of his toes to the frostbite of the streets. Hiep is used to these kind expressions, although he does not understand them. No matter - Thank you !

We are at the Federal Building in Boston - Office of Citizenship and Immigration. For the fourth time! The incompetence! We are here again to secure - come hell or high water - the documentation that Hiep lost twenty nine years ago. Essential documentation, documents without which one stays on the streets! And so there has been no access to social services, to money, to food, to health care, to shelter. Last week when she began her assessment through a Vietnamese interpreter, the psychiatrist asked Hiep: "what are you worried about". "I lost my identification" he immediately answered. We go through the metal detector line, I gesture to Hiep that he will not have to take off his belt like I had to – his is a rope. The stern looking Homeland Security Guards are at ease with him. Thank you ! he says to them. They smile, no one says that to them.

Immigration Officer Jones asks to see the white paper that she says she gave us the last visit. When I tell her that she did not give us a white paper, she grimaces - same as she did when she met us the first time, when she said: "I have been working without a break for eight hours." I try to mask my displeasure at Officer Jones - Hiep is calm. She tells us to come back again in three weeks. I say: "but how do we know that the file will be here then?' Officer Jones shrugs her shoulders. She is not pleased with me; I am not pleased with her. To Hiep with a smile she says some nice things. He understands none of it. But - Thank you !

And so ---After 29 years on the streets, I am thankful that Hiep is a new, growing, hopeful person. We are all amazed at how little he needs, how little he spends of his new social security money. He has shared that he is saving for a used car. And it will happen. Thank you !

∽

The Scarlet Letters

- She's left the shelter, I never had the opportunity to know her, never had the chance to offer therapy. Very few across the country get therapy on the streets for the scarlet letters. Perhaps our paths will cross again and I'll have another chance – lots that I am curious about .... is it harder for the women? What are the effects of sixteen years in prison, and the last six months in solitary confinement ?

- He cried when the DA investigator told him not to count on getting out, that he may be spending many more years in prison, maybe for the rest of his life even though he had completed his sentence. He was relieved when the judge found in his favor. Not used to people coming to his aide and not used to giving thanks – he thanked me and his lawyer for proving that it would be unlikely that he would offend again. I had hoped that he would keep in touch, I have not heard from him ....

- It took a while to learn to just let him rile, I had to get used to his hypervigilance and posturing. They said he was a malnourished fetal alcohol kid, he is still small but now wiry street built. He goes about his days doing the best that he can, mostly alone until recently – he has a girlfriend, it seems to

work for both of them. Departing from my protocol, I had
no need to know the particulars, because in the presence of
his therapist I was assured by her competence and her saying
that he is doing the work. The Administrative Law Judge
treated him with disdain and found that he is not disabled.
Were facts thrown out in deference to the scarlet letters?
So now we are knocking on the federal court house door.

• Strange, this fundamentalist shelter makes no distinctions,
they did not close their door to him and they asked me to see
him because he seemed in mental distress. It is obvious that he
has a low IQ. He realizes that people look at him differently
these days and he doesn't know why.

• He found Buddhism during his years in prison, said that it
changed his life. I thought this to be a good thing, we would have
a common thread as I know a little about Buddhism. It came to
the place where he said that if I brought up,"the subject" again,
there would be nothing to talk about. I felt no inner peace in
such an expression. And so we have nothing to talk about.

• He avoids everyone by always wearing ear phones – listening
to music while taking in everything around him and looking
straight ahead. Age forty. No one in his large family will talk
to him or see him. He told me that he is sorry – that he has
some understanding as to why he did it … drugs and alcohol
were a big part. He is feeling absolutely hopeless - has no
hope of getting a job and little hope of getting a place to live
outside of the shelter. No friends. We have met often, it is
always hard for him to go into the dark side, but he does. And
always the earphones- a very thin life line.

- It took me some time to allow myself to get to know this man, he looked like someone who in the past I would have envisioned dangerous : bulbous drinker's nose, penetrating eyes, no smile, gray / yellowish scruffy mustache and goatee, dirty long stringy hair on the sides - bald on the top with sprouts. Turned out to be a man sensitive to others, who clearly saw the crime ; who sees the value of treatment – did it while in prison and now with the Veteran's Administration. He remembers his many years in the Air Force - proud of that. He is not drinking and that is good.

- A tobacco farmer form Maine – was a model prisoner. It's been a year now, longest ever for not drinking. Goes to AA meetings, that surprised me .. They yell obscenities at him as they speed by. A big breakthrough was his exploring the feelings that he has for men – that he is gay. Elder Maine tobacco farmers don't come out. He has learned much, he's asked the good questions even though they are hard to get out.

- Perhaps because he is deaf, my exploration was slow and weak. On the other hand my instincts told me that I needed to be patient. He's convinced that "it was a one time thing" and that now with his religious conversion, it would not happen again. He's gone, out of state and I'm concerned.

- A carpenter, drinking explains his stay at the shelter. Outwardly he is sure of himself – cocky, intelligent, engaging. Did not see himself like "them" in the shelter. Our engagement stopped when I told him that what was overheard between he and his wife called for me to report child abuse. Several years later I saw him on the streets - we chatted, he spoke of growth and he looked healthier. And several years later I saw him again on the streets - intoxicated. In a sincere way he told me of his "propensity"…that he was concerned, that he was telling me – only me. There was no time or opportunity for us to talk further – no ties anymore, no time to get an address. I searched out where he might live – in a shelter again perhaps.

- "He had a fever, I was just holding him on my lap". Another one of the simple, "high functioning". He was a good auto body helper. In a shelter now, postered at city hall ; miles away from his hometown, on the bracelet, lost, confused, sad, alone and lonely.

- Another one who has chosen not to talk about "it". We did begin talking when he was under court orders – he skirted around "it" and said no – stopped after he wrapped up his sentence-now under no obligation. Unlike others who have taken a similar path, it was not easy for me to just let him go. I sensed that even though he protested, he wants the help. Others say that for the time being it is best to help him through any of his other crisis – kicked out of shelters, losing jobs, heroin, depression, worrying about his mother's health. No, in my gut and clinical experience says that I must pull him. Period. I saw him yesterday - "I need the therapy, but not about *that*".. I shrugged my shoulders, smiled and walked on. We'll meet again.

- He blurted out his hatred of her for putting him in prison and his determination to get back. I could feel the textbook, "… it's all about power and control" and now I have witnessed the "less than 1 percent are the very dangerous.". I have a duty to warn.

SA ... SO ... sexual abusers, sexual offenders ... the Scarlet Letters

And so...I'll do the work

True Love Waits

I done killed it – a half pint – schnapps, and I was fixing to kill the other when Richard the social worker pulled up. Knew what he was fixing to do, and I was ok with it - to take me to the hospital and then to detox. He and my two new women friends - Patsy and Barbara – they've been sticking by me but like Richard said "if he wants to drink, he'll find a way". I left the nooner – the AA meeting -, should have stayed, and went to the Country Jeweler and showed him Maggie's gold ring. I guess when I took it off her finger Saturday morning before the funeral people came, I knew what I was a fixing to do with it. My best friend, for twenty five years, and I knew what I was a fixing to do with the wedding ring that I gave her. The jeweler man gave me $ 40 dollars, said that he wouldn't take the silver one off my finger, said he remembered selling it to Maggie, that she said it was for her husband – he remembered doing the engraving, "true *love waits*". I asked Maggie when she gave me the ring why it wasn't gold – "because you might hock it for drink". Maggie she quit ten years ago. She just stopped, said she had enough and she never drank again. Never went to meetings or anything, Maggie was like that. She wanted me to quit real bad. When I'd do bad things, like get to her social security money and use it to drink, I'd say "are you mad at me ?" "No" she always said, "Just disappointed – *true loves waits*".

The landlord in Florida told us that we'd have to move – that people were complaining about Maggie's noise at night. I told him that she was in pain, a lot at night and that I was trying to get help, but couldn't. So I said let's get to your sister's, in Massachusetts. So we left – she in the broken wheelchair and with the oxygen. And when we got to her sister's she was in *real* pain and the sister said get her to the hospital - I wheeled her up there. I never been away from her, they let me stay a night but no more. They got me into the shelter. Me and Maggie been in that shelter before, years ago. That shelter was so far from Maggie, I didn't know what to do. I walked each day to see her and one day she was gone and that scared me. They told me that she was at a nursin home – Poets Seat. I walked there, she didn't look better and they told me that she wouldn't eat and that she was asking for me.

I met Richard, the social worker, in the shelter hallway – said smiling that it was his office. He listened and then asked me if Maggie – Maggie and I – if we had thought about Hospice. That scared me, I knew what it was, so did Maggie what with she being a nurse aide and all. And I knew then, by his saying it, that my Maggie was dying - my heart was breaking. We talked with people at the nursin home, they told me that she was in pain but she did not want to make any decisions – that she trusted me to make them. I didn't want to make any decisions. When I first was with her - just she and I - she said 'Mike, don't let me die". I told her that I couldn't promise that – I wanted to be honest. She just wasn't eatin … sometimes, only when I was there next to her, she'd take a little, mostly sips of coffee. The nursin home people told me that we needed to talk, that they knew it would be hard for me. They told me that because she wasn't eatin, she probably would die soon. That broke my heart, my heart is breaking.

Richard asked if I'd like him to see Maggie with me there, I said I'd like that. They didn't say much, he just said hello, that he was a social worker and he'd be watching out for me. Maggie usually doesn't care much for men – but she took to him, I could tell.

We talked about cremation and about where we would bury Maggie, about letting her relatives know … things about her dying. My heart was breaking – and I wanted to drink. Richard asked me if I'd like to see the place where if I wanted to we could bury Maggie. I was surprised that I said yes and glad that we had a cup of coffee in a small coffee place on the way – and that I could smoke in his car. Drinking the coffee, the music came, I knew it right away, said to Richard, "this is Maggie's favorite song … Tears in Heaven – Erik Clapton –" will you know me when you see me in heaven ?"

My heart was breaking. And I wanted to drink. In the cemetery, with us sittin on a small stone bench with the mountains all around us, Richard told me that he thought that Maggie was in pain and that she was holding on 'cause she did not want to leave me and that it would be good if we talked about it … that Hospice would take care of the pain. I told him maybe; I liked the cemetery – peaceful. That same afternoon I told Maggie. "Maggie, I'll be all right, I don't want you to be in anymore pain - I'll be all right". She whispered to me to put my head next to her, and I did for a good while – just she and I - I was crying. She signed the paper.

People came to watch with me – she was dying. A nurse from the shelter, Patsy, Barbara, two people who worked in the nursin home who took a likin to Maggie. In the early morning it was just Richard and I. Maggie put her hands together like she was a fixing to pray, I said "do you want to pray?" She did a little point to the window – the shelf under it, and it came to me. Her bible! I put her bible next to her. She smiled. I got real close, she whispered that she was going to Jesus. I told her that I loved her and she squeezed my hand… A little while later the breathing came to a rattling, but no pain. I could tell when she passed over because Richard had his arms out.

The pastor said that it was the nicest grave side service that he had ever been to. My new friend Barbara, Richard and I put it together. I'll be sending the program that we made to relatives, the picture that I made for Maggie with the four colored roses, that's on the front, says - "You will be in my … and there I drew a heart – forever. Love Mike". I just did not know if I could lower her ashes into the hole, I did.

Three days later I got drunk - that's another story, got a lot to do with that being the date that Maggie picked me up hitchhiking. As I wait to get into the Emergency Room to be what they call medically cleared on my way to detox I'm crying cause I ripped up that program – I am so mad at Maggie's leaving me. Barbara reminded me that we have more of them; maybe Maggie didn't mind, just disappointed and saying, "True *love waits*".

And so … I am not the same.

∞

Dust of Snow

It was the second snow of the season, snow upon snow, a dusting.
I liked it; I've accepted snow in my life, we are friends - I am
always dressed for it. Joannah – it took me a while to write her
name, with an h and at the end - Joannah was not dressed for
it. Her unzipped coat was a winter thing, but just on the fringe
of a winter thing. Like she has said of herself: "I am just on the
fringe". A pain to do all of those tasks from a wheelchair, forget
about zipping up a coat. "Shit" she easily says when the papers,
folders, books, lose their hold and fly from her lap. She allows
me to pick up the whatever – only because there is no choice. A
delicate thing this allowing people to help the cripple. Last week
she bit the head off of a nice person who was about to assist her
with a push up the ramp. And she knew that she bit … and had
regrets … but forgave herself and moved on. Holding her tongue
is not something that she does well these days. Some think that
she should be eternally grateful that she has been allowed to stay
in this respite facility, and that she has not been relegated to a
nursing home – again - or pushed to go to some homeless shelter
that does not exist for folks in wheelchairs.   And there is the daily
pressure for her to make the time line capitalized in the e- mail,
THIRTY DAYS.   Do they feel that she is less of a priority among
all the broken people? Broken is broken. Do they not know
how hard it is these days for her to just do the smallest of tasks?

Movin - movin - movin … keep those doggies movin ! She is not deferential - such an ingrate: "Here we are in 2012, twenty plus years after the passage of The American with Disabilities Act, and I can barely get my wheel chair up this ramp, and because the bars are not right, I may well tip over … and I have not taken a bath in five days, why do they keep removing the fucking shower chair ?" Does she fear that *she* is becoming inaccessible?

I came to know her four weeks ago when a respite worker knowing of what I do – a dog with a bone - called me and asked me to see Dr. Whitney. Oh yes, *Dr*, an Anthropologist / Archeologist - PhD. PhD slash / Street Person. I know how challenging this journey will be but I do not let her know, my job is to give her reason to hope – she showed me her fear of returning to a nursing home --- black and blue thighs from self inflicted poundings. I assured her that her next move would be going to her own apartment - going to the "least restrictive environment" is a social work value, notwithstanding the incidentals of time constraints, limited housing opportunities, even less available '"handicapped" apartments, no money, few supports.

"Age one, age two, age three … "my assessments take about an hour; they let me see a whole person. And I will not share. If you are curious as to how she became "chronically homeless"… imagine the unexpected things that could easily go wrong in your life. I read today of a returning Vet whose face has been burned – really burned - and of the good work that doctors are doing for him. Of greater import is to know that she has refused to be cast aside, that she has never lost the expectation – *expectation* not hope - that in the near future she will return to what she is called to do and that because of this experience that call will be more obvious.

Today our tasks centered on the Winslow House run by the Housing Authority. It has just been rehabilitated and there is a "handicapped" apartment which appears nice. We have dropped off reams of papers, including an emergency application. After bringing the wheel chair to her, with snow falling lightly, she is seated next to me - still with coat unzipped and with even more stuff perilously upon her lap, waiting for us to move. Because she and her chair are in front of me, I have to extend and slam the door – I do not like slamming. From the top of my hood, snow flakes came flying … showering us. I liked it – startling and gentle. Then my thought went to her, attached to the earth but unable to even pretend that she could move out of harms way. I lamented that I was not more thoughtful, more careful and said something to that effect. And she said in an instant:

> The way a crow
> Shook down on me
> The dust of snow
> From a hemlock tree
>
> Has given my heart
> A change of mood
> And saved some part
> Of a day I had rued

And so --- "Dust of Snow" by Robert Frost. And with close to trepidation I told her that some of the good people who used to live at the Winslow … when it was the seedy Harco … that they will be reapplying. How would this refined woman react day in and out to this cast of characters?   Later as we shared a meal at the Coop, I found her smiling out the window and then she gestured, "come in". She introduced me to Raphael. At that moment Raphael was very "street" -   behaviors that could be off putting. She responded to him with dignity and grace; as he staggered off, he blew her a kiss. She smiled and blew it back. She will do just fine at the Winslow.

What's in a Name?

Dear Siobhan Alanine Tristan Regan

I too, value saying a person's name correctly and understand your insistence that regardless of its difference, given time people need to learn to say yours. It took me a while but I am glad that I understood your chagrin and made the effort to get it right. I practiced it, particularly before meeting with you.

Siobhan Alanine Tristan Regan I was surprised when you looked up at me and easily said, "so when are you going to write the book?" And pleased at your widened lovely eyes when I answered that I was about to push the button and send it off to the publisher. This work began with Gus Leady telling me to write and now ends by you affirming its value. Spiritual bookends for me. By clinical definition you are totally self - absorbed and should have no interest in another person. Another example of the wanting of science. Thanks for stepping out of your box *for me*.

I struggled with how I was going to talk to you about my findings to Social Security - a continuation of the struggle begun when I encouraged you to apply but warning that it would call for my doing a write up on "mental illness", and to boot, mental illness that is debilitating. Such a final word, "debilitating". Early on, in the shelter, I saw that your ways of going about things constantly got in your way, ending up hurting you - same as it did resulting in cutting you short of your theology degree. That continuously standing tall for yourself – appearing above ' those others', drew reactions from those living in the shelter and staff ; the perception was that you held them in sweet disdain. In my clinical bible there is a name, a label for this behavior, we have labels for all kinds of behaviors. You were calmer than I expected when I gave you the tag that I would be using in my write up:Narcissistic Personality Disorder:a preeminent love of self.

I was touched by how you saw this mental illness tag : "Look, if people cannot take the time to pronounce my name correctly that is their problem and it does not make me crazy… and by the way, I think that there is wisdom in first loving yourself - but hells bells, I'll go along if it will get me $ 700 a month for as long as I'm in this predicament." I see it as a tad more than an issue of name mispronunciation but I understand. Sad that we have to give folks labels and make them "disabled" when all they want is help.

I received word today that your application has been allowed. My write- up, the report of the consulting psychologist and the doctor in Worcester who makes the final decision, we all agree that your mental state keeps you from working… and *oh and incidentally,* that it has caused you much distress ! I refrain from congratulating you for this allowance … "And the winner in the category of narcissism is …"

Siobhan Alanine Tristan Regan, please, with this disability "allowance" do continue to thumb your nose at us who might think that we gave you what is your right, we are well intended and all in all do good work. Take our suggestions as to how to do the dance in a way that does not take you off the dance floor, but do not give in to denying who you are called to be, do not let go of your vision of who you are. The Trappist monk and spiritual writer Thomas Merton noted that a Saint is one who recognizes who one is - and in the words of Mr. Rogers, "no one else is like you, you are special ... and I like you just the way that you are". So do I.

Be well Siobhan Alanine Tristan Regan and keep insisting that we get it right.

And so ... I like it when people use my name ; most on the streets call me Richard, few in my other world call me anything. The next time I'm out of uniform in Boston and giving some change, I'll ask the person to share their name, and I'll give them mine. A name is not inconsequential, it's the door to a person.

David

_____

She said of her bedroom, "No other furniture, just this bed!"

We have prevailed - jumped through the hoops, battled the systems. The landlord put in new carpeting and painted the walls white. Although there are many things on her to do list, it smells new, looks new and after 25 years on the streets – *she has a key*! We had our variety of tears as that small key was handed to her.

Looking in on the bedroom, I had the same reaction in Venice when standing in front of Michangelo's David - Fixated. We looked in reverent silence for minute. I whispered, "it's beautiful!" The new bed. I've taken to calling it David.

David,- a large, low, top of the line, wood bordered, "I am grounded and going nowhere" futon. 24 karat gold-like sheets. Gold pillow cases covering large pillows; and graced on top, a white embroidered bedspread made by a friend - daisies.

There have been other beds---

The bed of the Mother - never allowed

The bed of the Father with child daughter

The bed of relatives and foster homes

The bed of the Father with adolescent daughter

The bed of the Father with teenage daughter

The bed of all- night convenience stores, park benches, friends

The bed of the Father with adult daughter

The bed of the woods - of soup kitchens, tricks, jail cells, ambulances, hospitals, respite

The bed of psychiatric wards, crack houses, detoxes, therapists

The bed on the pew in front of Mary

The bed over the grate, under the bridge, on overstuffed chairs at Starbucks

But now, now - - - DAVID

And so --- She will never heal completely … but now one day at a time she may sleep

TAPS

They said that she was *extremely* distrustful. We met, I said
Hi - Heidi gave me her hand – our beginning. The hand given
perhaps because she knew that I was not judging and that I'd been
around the block. Wanting to hear her – and intrigued by the
proliferation of her body accoutrements.

When I came to know that she was a gifted trumpeter, I asked
her how she could play with hardware on her lips. She smiled
and in an instant tucked them out of the way. Voila! That's how!
Tufts of orange spiked hair, chain, many of the tattoos broken
up by pale scars - the result of cutting for release of pain. And
the fresh pink scar across her neck that advertised the recent
attempt.

I saw no circus. We met four times; each conversation
challenging, insightful and delightful. Heidi was impressed that I
play the bugle and that I know the words to Taps– she said that she
always wanted to get them. I got them to her the next day – she
smiled.

She moved on the following day. I think to a safe place. I pray so.

And so---Day is done, gone the sun,
from the lakes, from the hills from the sky
all is well, safely rest God is neigh.
Be well my friend.

Horton and I on a break next to the soup kitchen in the outdoor Dr. Seuss Museum.

Richard Hendrick, MSW, LICSW

I've been doing social work in the settlement house tradition for many years, the last fifteen helping people who have no homes – helping in the city, in the country , in soup kitchens, shelters, alleys, abandoned buildings, day centers, clinics ... in flower pots – helping on the streets, on buses, on park benches. And what is next?

"So … be your name Baxbaum or Bixby or Bray or Mordecai Ali Van Allen O'Shea, you're off to great places! Today is your day! Your mountain is waiting, so…get on your way!" Dr. Seuss, Poet (Oh, the places you'll go!)